IN ESSENCE

EVOLVE YOUR VISION · CHANGE YOUR WORLD

HIS DIVINE GRACE
A. C. BHAKTIVEDANTA SWAMI PRABHUPĀDA
Founder-*Ācārya* of the International Society
for Krishna Consciousness

THE BHAKTIVEDANTA BOOK TRUST

Readers interested in the subject matter of
this book are invited to contact the International Society
for Krishna Consciousness (see address list in back of book)
or one of the following information centres:

ISKCON Reader Services UK
Tel. +44 (0)1923 851000
readerservices@pamho.net
krishnawisdom.com
info@krishnawisdom.com

ISKCON Reader Services Ireland
Tel. +44 (0)28 6772 3878
tp@krishnaisland.com

To order any of our books, go to blservices.com

In Essence was compiled from the books,
lectures, and room conversations of His Divine Grace
A. C. Bhaktivedanta Swami Prabhupāda
by Sutapa Dāsa and Kaiśorī Devī Dāsī.

Cover by Prasannatma Dasa (Prashant Malur)

MIX
Paper from responsible sources
FSC® C083411
FSC www.fsc.org
The mark of responsible forestry

bbt.se
bbt.org
bbtmedia.com
krishna.com

ISBN 978-91-7769-088-7

Printed in 2019

A complimentary ebook of this title is available at
bbtmedia.com • Code: **EB16EN86542P**

Contents

	Introduction	vii
1	The Inside Story	1
2	Designing Your Destiny	9
3	The Lord of Attraction	25
4	The Love Vacuum	37
5	Honest Religion Defined	47
6	Yoga 101	55
7	Bhakti Life	67
8	Yogic Perfection – Living the Dream	81
9	Essays	
	Teachings of the Vedas	91
	What is Kṛṣṇa Consciousness, or Bhakti-yoga?	101
	Who is Kṛṣṇa?	107
	The Six Benefits of Practising Bhakti-yoga	113
	How to Practise Bhakti-yoga	123

Śrīla Prabhupāda 137
Glossary 143
Guide to Sanskrit Pronunciation 147

Introduction

'The important thing is not to stop questioning; curiosity has its own reason for existing.'

– Albert Einstein

This book is for seekers. We human beings have been trying to understand our world since the beginning of time. Philosophers, theologians and scientists have also tried to interpret the world for us. But we still wonder why we're here and whether our lives have meaning. What future awaits our children and grandchildren? Will there ever be peace? And more privately, we wonder why love hurts or never seems to last, why bad things happen to us even though we're basically good people and whether we'll find lasting happiness before we die.

These existential questions confront each of us at some point in our lives, and most of us will feel compelled, at some point, to answer them. Reading this book is a good place to start. Here we present questions asked over the years by other seekers. We drew our answers from the books, conversations, and lectures of His Divine Grace A.C. Bhaktivedanta Swami Prabhupāda (1896–1977), founder-*ācārya* and spiritual master of the Hare Kṛṣṇa movement. Śrīla Prabhupāda, as his students affectionately called him, was a philosopher, scholar, social revolutionary and the pioneer who brought the Hare Kṛṣṇa mantra, now sung in yoga meditation sessions around the globe, and the wisdom tradition of bhakti-yoga to the Western world. (His astonishing story is told in brief starting on p. 137.)

Śrīla Prabhupāda was a bhakti-yogi, a practitioner of the yoga of service and devotion. About one in ten of us are now practising some form of yoga – double the number of just a few years ago – and although most people begin their yoga practice with hatha-yoga in order to better their health, many gradually discover yoga's deeper, spiritual aspects. Bhakti-yoga is the heart of the yoga tradition.

Why has yoga become so popular? First, it's because happiness is, of course, everyone's concern. Secondly, happiness is more easily found in a life of balance and harmony, of being in sync with ourselves, one another, our world and the source of our existence, and that's what yoga – particularly bhakti-yoga – is all about.

So Śrīla Prabhupāda answers the questions in this book from the viewpoint of a bhakti-yogi, speaking from texts such as the *Bhagavad-gītā,* one of yoga's primary philosophical works, and the *Śrīmad-Bhāgavatam,* the philosophical and literary exposition on bhakti philosophy.

You have the power to make your life happier, less stressful and more centred on what matters. We are always doing things – working, playing, dancing, learning, looking at things, sleeping, eating ... we're endlessly active. Who are you underneath all that busy-ness? Are you the body you see when you look in the mirror, or is that body simply yours? If you're not that body, then who are you? Opening mind and heart to that sort of exploration can let you see the world and everything in it differently. Let this book help you take a step on your journey inward.

Start where this book starts, with the most essential and existential question – 'Who am I?' – or flip through and find questions and answers that speak to you. If you find yourself intrigued and would like to know more about bhakti-yoga, Śrīla Prabhupāda or any of the topics discussed here, we'd love to hear from you: info@krishnawisdom.com.

In his speaking from the bhakti tradition, Śrīla Prabhupāda peppered his talks and writings with Sanskrit terms. To make this book easier to read, we have translated or glossed these terms in the question-and-answer section but left them intact in 'A Short Compendium of Śrīla Prabhupāda's Writings'. For those who are interested in how to pronounce any of the Sanskrit words in this book, there's a handy pronunciation guide at the end, and we've also included a glossary.

1

The Inside Story

The urge to find pleasure underpins everything we do. Capitalizing on this very human pursuit, we've been systematically programmed by society to pursue satisfaction through romance, sports, the arts, education, our professions and almost every other activity. Yet we're often left with feelings of frustration and emptiness. Even when we do find enjoyment, the sensation quickly fades and we all too quickly return to the ordinariness of our lives, leaving us looking for the next new thing in which to invest our hopes.

The Bhagavad-gītā challenges us to seek a quality of happiness beyond our current limitations. The Gītā's fundamental teaching is that we're spiritual beings inhabiting material bodies. So self-satisfaction requires knowing who that self is. And that requires looking beyond the temporary matters that dominate our attention to what actually concerns us. That's the inside story: if we're serious about finding lasting happiness, we have to start with knowing who we are.

Who am I?

The first lesson of Vedic wisdom is that we are not bodies but rather spirit souls – minute particles of consciousness dwelling within the body and animating it. Just as a car is a machine that allows a driver to travel from point A to point B, the body is a machine that allows the spirit soul to act and to experience sensations and thoughts within the Lord's material nature.

Why is this the first lesson?

We are all hankering for complete self-satisfaction, *ātma-suprasāda,* but first we must know what the real self is. The word *ātmā,* or 'self', refers to the body, the mind and the soul. Actually, we are the spirit soul covered by two kinds of 'garments'. Just as a gentleman is covered by his shirt and coat, so I, the soul, am covered by a gross body consisting of the physical senses and a subtle body consisting of mind, intelligence and false ego. A person covered by false ego identifies with the body. When asked who he is, he will answer, 'I am an American' or 'I am an Indian', etc. But these are bodily designations; they are not his real identity.

The Vedic literature teaches that we begin to understand our real identity when we think, 'I am spirit soul.' Therefore the *Vedānta-sūtra* says, 'Now one should inquire about spirit.' The human form of life is meant for advancing in knowledge of spirit, and this knowledge is the beginning of real happiness.

How can I be a soul? I can't see the soul, and science has never found evidence that souls exist.

Even a man completely ignorant of the spiritual nature can somehow feel its presence. One need only analyse his body silently: 'What am I? Am I this finger? Am I this body? Am I this hair? No, I am not this and I am not that. I am something other than this body. I am something beyond this body. What is that? That is the spiritual.' In this way, we can feel or sense the presence of spirituality within this matter. We can sense the absence of spirit when a body is dead. If we witness someone dying, we can sense that something is leaving the body. Although we do not have the eyes to see it, that something is spirit. Its presence in the body is explained in the very beginning of the *Bhagavad-gītā* (2.17): 'Know that which pervades the entire body to be indestructible. No one is able to destroy the imperishable soul.'

Because we cannot perceive the soul with our gross senses we deny its existence. Actually, there are so many things we cannot see with our blunt senses. We cannot see air, radio waves or sound, nor can we perceive minute bacteria. But this does not mean they are not there. By the aid of the microscope and other instruments, many things can be perceived which the imperfect senses had previously denied. Just because the soul, which is atomic in size, has not yet been perceived by our senses or instruments, that does not mean we should conclude that it is not there. The soul can be perceived by its symptoms and effects.

Can you tell me more about the soul?

This living spirit remains within the body just like a tiny dose of a potent medicine: the soul spreads its presence all over the body. And thus we can understand that the sensitivity we experience to even the slightest touch on any part of the body is due to the spreading of this living spirit throughout the body. But when this minute quantity of living spark is gone from the body, the body lies dead, prostrate, and it cannot feel the slightest pain, even if hacked by an axe.

That this minute living spark, the spirit, is not a material thing is proved by the fact that no material scientist has ever been able to create the living spark by any combination or quantity of material substances. Experienced material scientists have been obliged to accept the fact that the living spark cannot be duplicated by material science. Whatever can be created by the manipulation of matter is destructible and temporary. In contrast, the living spark is indestructible precisely because it can never be constructed by any combination or quantity of matter. We can produce material atomic bombs, but not the spiritual spark of life.

How does knowing this change my life?

Suppose you have a nice coat. If you simply show the coat and iron the coat and keep it very carefully, you'll never be happy. Similarly, now you are trying to get happiness from gratifying the coat of the body, but that is not possible. Happiness comes only when you make the soul happy. Or, suppose you have a bird in a cage. If you simply polish the cage but do not give the bird any food, the bird will never be happy. Similarly, the material body is the cage of the soul, and if we simply care for the body, the soul will never become happy. So, the beginning of spiritual knowledge is to understand that the soul is encaged within the body and mind and that neither bodily comforts nor mental satisfaction will ever bring the soul real happiness.

Isn't the mind part of the soul?

No, the mind is not the soul but an instrument through which the soul acts. The mind is rejecting and accepting according to the dictations of the soul. Although I walk with my legs, I do not consider myself to *be* my legs. Although I think with my mind, I am not my mind. Some philosophers identify the mind with the self, and this is a mistake. Intelligence is subtler than the mind, and the mind is subtler than the senses. The gross senses can be seen, but the centre of the senses, the mind, cannot be seen. Therefore it is called subtle. The mind is guided by the intelligence, which is even subtler. The background of that intelligence is the soul. The mind is the instrument by which we think, but that instrument is not 'I'.

I see plenty of happy people who aren't spiritual. How do you explain that?

Because the fire of knowledge is not burning in our minds, we accept material existence as happiness. A dog or hog cannot understand what kind of miserable life he is passing. He actually thinks that he is enjoying life, and this is called the covering or illusive influence of material energy.

We may be in a miserable condition, but we accept it, thinking that we are very happy. This is called ignorance. But when one is awakened to knowledge, he thinks, 'Oh, I am not happy. I want freedom, but there is no freedom. I don't want to die, but there is death. I don't want to grow old, but there is old age. I don't want diseases, but there are diseases.' These are the major problems of human existence, but we ignore them and concentrate on solving very minor problems. We consider economic development to be the most important thing, forgetting how long we shall live here in this material world. Economic development or no economic development, at the end of sixty or a hundred years our life will be finished. Even if we accumulate a million dollars, we must leave it all behind when we leave this body. We need to come to understand that in the material world whatever we are doing is being defeated by the influence of material nature.

Are you saying material happiness is not real happiness?

Every one of us is searching after happiness, but we do not know what real happiness is. We see so much advertised about happiness, but practically speaking we see so few happy people. This is because so few people know that the platform of real happiness is beyond temporary things. It is this real happiness that is described in the *Bhagavad-gītā* by Lord Kṛṣṇa to Arjuna.

To cite an example I have given many times, if you take a fish out of water, you can give it a very comfortable velvet bedstead, but still the fish cannot be happy; it will die. Because the fish is an animal of the water, it cannot be happy without water. Similarly, we are all spirit soul; unless we are in spiritual life or in the spiritual world, we cannot be happy. That is our position.

But what if I am satisfied with my standard of happiness?

If one asks a tree, 'Are you feeling happy?' the tree, if it could, might say, 'Yes, I am happy standing here all year. I'm enjoying the wind and snowfall very much.' This may be enjoyed by the tree, but for the human being it is a very low standard of enjoyment. There are different kinds and grades of living entities, and their conceptions and perceptions of happiness are also of all different types and grades. Although one animal may see that another animal is being slaughtered, he will go right on chewing grass, for he has no knowledge to understand that he may be next. He is thinking that he is happy, but at the next moment he may be slaughtered. In this way there are different degrees of happiness. Yet of all of them, what is the highest happiness? Śrī Kṛṣṇa tells Arjuna in the *Bhagavad-gītā* (6.21): 'In that joyous state [*samādhi*], one is situated in boundless transcendental happiness and enjoys himself through transcendental senses. Established thus, one never departs from the truth.'

In the desert there is no water, but the foolish deer runs after illusory water in the desert to quench his thirsty heart. Water is not unreal, but the place where we seek it is misleading. The advancement of materialistic civilization is just like a mirage in the desert. The deer runs after water in the desert with full speed, and the illusion of water moves ahead at the same speed as the foolish deer. Water is not false, but we must not seek it in the desert. A living entity, by his past experience, remembers the real happiness of his original, spiritual existence, but since he has forgotten himself he seeks spiritual or permanent happiness in matter, although this is impossible to achieve.

There are ways to measure happiness. One is by how intense the pleasure is. Another is its duration. Another is whether we can depend on an experience to produce pleasure. Another is how immediately we feel the pleasure. Another is whether the pleasure creates other pleasures, or will our happy experiences end in pain? Is there any pain mixed in with our pleasure? And can our pleasure be shared? If we use this standard to test material happiness, we'll understand there is no happiness. This test shows it is impossible to get happiness in the material world.

Isn't this a rather bleak, pessimistic view of the world?

It is said that we are passing through an age of darkness called Kali-yuga. What is this darkness? The darkness cannot be due to backwardness in material knowledge because we now have more material knowledge than we had formerly. Therefore we must conclude that the darkness of the present age is not due to a lack of material advancement but that we have lost the clue to our spiritual advancement, which is the prime necessity of human life and the criterion of the highest type of human civilization. Throwing bombs from airplanes is not an advance from the primitive, uncivilized practice of dropping big stones on the heads of enemies from the tops of hills. Improvement in the art of killing our neighbours by means of machine guns and poisonous gases is certainly not an advance from primitive barbarism, which prided itself on its art of killing with bows and arrows. Nor does the development of a sense of pampered selfishness prove anything more than intellectual animalism.

All of us are spiritual entities. We cannot have perfect happiness, which is our birthright, however much we may meddle with the affairs of mundane things. Perfect happiness can be ours only when we are restored to our natural state of spiritual existence.

What do you mean by 'intellectual animalism'?

Civilization attempts to improve eating, sleeping, mating and defence, but these are not the real problems. A man sleeps and a dog sleeps. A man is not more advanced simply because he has a nice apartment in which to sleep. In both cases, the business is the same: sleeping. Man has discovered atomic weapons for defence, but the dog also has teeth and claws and can defend itself. In both cases, defence is there. Man cannot say that because he has the atomic bomb he can conquer the entire world or the entire universe. That is not possible. Man may possess an elaborate method for defence, or a gorgeous method for eating, sleeping or mating, but that does not make him advanced. We may call his advancement polished animalism, that is all.

So how should we use our intelligence?

In the various forms of life lower than human life, the intelligence does not go beyond the range of life's primary necessities – namely eating, sleeping, mating and defending. Dogs, cats and tigers are always busy trying to find something to eat or a place to sleep, trying to defend and have sexual intercourse successfully. In the human form of life, however, one should be intelligent enough to ask what he is, why he has come into the world, what his duty is, who is the supreme controller, what is the difference between dull matter and the living entity, etc. There are so many questions, and the person who is actually intelligent should simply inquire about the supreme source of everything.

2

Designing Your Destiny

Our daily lives are like a drama at the theatre. We assume the role of the protagonist, and others take on the parts of our parents, friends, lovers and foes. But who are we when we're 'offstage'? And when the curtain falls and death comes, what becomes of us and everyone else who had roles in our theatrical play?

This chapter discusses, among other things, karma and reincarnation and how the individual, the conscious soul, moves from one body to another only to create a new drama.

Shakespeare was right when he said, 'All the world's a stage.' The world's a stage on which we must serve the desires of others and seek to fulfil our own. Like any drama, our lives are divided into scenes, and how we choose to play each scene shapes our destiny – all our future scenes. Each scene also contains life lessons taught through the action-reaction cycles of karma, the universal law of cause and effect from which none of us are exempt. Karma indicates that we are responsible for our actions, and reincarnation indicates that that responsibility doesn't end with the death of the physical body. This cosmic education teaches us why bad things happen to good people (and good things happen to bad people). Ultimately, it should awaken us to the truth of ourselves as souls and our relationship with the world around us. Learning our karmic lessons well moves us closer to the eternal, unchanging, absolute, self-manifest, blissful and personal nature of the soul and our relationship with our Source. Our life has meaning inasmuch as we endeavour to reconnect with both these truths.

What happens when we die?

The *Bhagavad-gītā* (2.22) states, 'As a person puts on new garments, giving up old ones, the soul similarly accepts new material bodies, giving up the old and useless ones.' When a coat is old and cannot be used anymore, one has to purchase another. The man is the same, but his clothes are supplied according to the price he can pay. Similarly, you 'purchase' a new body with the 'money', or karma, you have accumulated in your life. According to your karma you receive a certain type of body.

The body is changing – from one form to another – but the spirit soul exists eternally without change. We can experience this fact in our own lives. Since the beginning of our material body in the womb of our mother, our body has been changing from one shape to another at every second and at every minute. This process is generally known as 'growth', but actually it is a change of body.

On this earth we see the change of day and night and of the seasons. The more primitive mentality attributes this phenomenon to changes occurring in the sun. For example, in the winter, primitive people think the sun is getting weaker, and at night they presume, sometimes, that the sun is dead. With more advanced knowledge, we see that the sun is not changing at all in this way. Seasonal and diurnal changes are attributed to the change of the relative positions of the earth and the sun.

Similarly, we experience bodily changes – from embryo to child to youth to maturity to old age to death. The less intelligent mentality presumes that after death the spirit soul's existence is forever finished, just as primitive tribes believe that the sun dies at sunset. Actually, however, the sun is rising in another part of the world. Similarly, the soul is accepting another type of body. When the body gets old like an old garment and is no longer usable, the soul accepts another body, just as we accept a new suit of clothes. Modern civilization is practically unaware of this truth.

There are different departments of knowledge in different universities and many technological institutions, all to study and understand the subtle laws of material nature, and there are medical research laboratories to study the physiological condition of the material body, but there is no institution to study the constitutional position of the soul. This is the greatest drawback of materialistic civilization, which is simply an external manifestation of the soul.

Can you explain what karma is?

From time immemorial, the living entity travels in the different species of life and the different planets, almost perpetually. This process is explained in the *Bhagavad-gītā* (18.61): under the spell of illusion, everyone is wandering throughout the universe on the carriage of the body offered by the material energy. Materialistic life involves a series of actions and reactions. It is a long film spool of actions and reactions, and one lifespan is just a flash in such a reactionary show. When a child is born, it is to be understood that his particular type of body is the beginning of another set of activities, and when an old man dies, it is to be understood that one set of reactionary activities is finished.

We can see that because of different reactionary activities, one man is born in a rich family and another is born in a poor family, although both of them are born in the same place, at the same moment and in the same atmosphere. One who is carrying pious activity with him is given a chance to take his birth in a rich or pious family, and one who is carrying impious activity is given a chance to take birth in a lower, poor family. The change of body means a change to a different field of activities.

It is clear that a particular body is given to the living entity for a particular type of activity. This process is going on perpetually, from a time that is impossible to trace out.

Can you explain how the soul moves from one body to the next?

All of us had at one time the body of a small baby. Where is that body? That body is gone. Presently I am an old man, but I remember that I was once a small baby. I still remember when I was about six months old; I was lying down on the lap of my elder sister, who was knitting, and I was playing. I can remember that, so it is possible for everyone to remember that he had a small body. After the baby's body I had a boy's body; then I had a youthful body, and now I am in this body. Where are those bodies? They are gone now. This is a different body. It is explained in the *Bhagavad-gītā* that when I give up this body I will have to accept another body. It is very simple to understand. I have changed so many bodies, not only from childhood to boyhood to youth, but according to medical science we are changing bodies every second, imperceptibly. This process indicates that the soul is permanent. Although I have changed many bodies, I remember my baby body and my childhood body – I am the same person, the soul.

Why do you keep talking about death?

As long as a man is in the full vigour of life, he forgets the naked truth of death, which he has to meet. Thus a foolish man makes no relevant inquiry about the real problems of life. Everyone thinks that he will never die, although he sees evidence of death before his eyes at every second. Here is the distinction between animalism and humanity. An animal like a goat has no sense of its impending death. Although its brother goat is being slaughtered, the goat, being allured by the green grass offered to it, will stand peacefully waiting to be slaughtered next. On the other hand, if a human being sees his fellow man being killed by an enemy, he either fights to save his brother or leaves, if possible, to save his own life. That is the difference between a man and a goat.

An intelligent man knows that death is born along with his own birth. He knows that he is dying at every second and that the final touch will be given as soon as his term of life is finished. He therefore prepares himself for the next life or for liberation from the disease of repeated birth and death.

Is what you're teaching from a particular religion?

Human civilization should be moulded so that people will have the chance to think soberly about the truth of life – to inquire about God, this material nature, our relationship with God and with nature and so on. That is called *tattva-jijñāsā,* inquiry into the Absolute Truth. It is everyone's duty to inquire into the Absolute Truth. There is no question of this being the duty of the Hindus but not the Muslims and the Christians. Truth is truth. That two plus two equals four is accepted by the Hindus, the Muslims, the Christians and everyone else. Science is science. Therefore everyone should be inquisitive about the science of the Absolute Truth.

Why is it that most people seem to miss this point?

We have succeeded in creating a humbug civilization. Every year so many cars are being manufactured, and for that purpose so many roads have to be excavated, prepared and repaired. This creates problem after problem, and therefore it is *māyā-sukhāya,* illusory happiness. We are trying to manufacture some way to be happy, but we only succeed in creating other problems. The United States has the world's largest number of cars, but that does not solve any problems. We have manufactured cars to help solve the problems of life, but we often experience that this also creates other problems. Once we create cars, we must travel thirty or forty miles just to meet our friends or go to a doctor. We can even go from New York to Boston in less than an hour by plane, but it takes even longer than that just to get to the airport. This situation is called *māyā-sukhāya*. *Māyā* means false, illusory. We try to create a very comfortable situation, but we only succeed in creating another uncomfortable situation. This is the way of the material world; if we are not satisfied by the natural comforts offered by God and nature, and we want to create artificial comforts, then we have to create discomfort also. Most people, ignorant of this fact, think that they are creating a very comfortable situation, but in actuality they end up travelling fifty miles to go to the office to earn a livelihood and fifty miles to come back.

The Indian political philosopher Cāṇakya Paṇḍita asks, 'Who is happy?' He answers, 'The man who does not work away from home and who is not a debtor – he is happy.' Very simple. Yet now we see that practically everyone works away from home and everyone is a great debtor. So how can they be happy? In America the banks canvass, 'Borrow money from us, purchase a motorcar, purchase a house, and as soon as you get your salary, give it to us.' Or they offer, 'Take this bank card.' It should be known as a bankrupt card. If you take the card and deposit your money in the bank, then you can purchase whatever you like with the card. But soon you are without any money, and all you have left is that card.

But hasn't science improved the world in many ways?

Once, a rat was being troubled by a cat, so the rat went to a saintly person who had mystic powers and said, 'My dear sir, I am very much troubled.'

'What is the difficulty?'

'A cat always chases me, so I have no peace of mind.'

'Then what do you want?'

'Please make me into a cat.'

'All right, become a cat.'

After a few days, the cat came to the saintly person and said, 'My dear sir, again I am in trouble.'

'What is that trouble?'

'The dogs are chasing me.'

'Then what do you want?'

'Make me a dog.'

'All right, become a dog.'

Then after a few days the dog came and said, 'Sir, again I am in trouble.'

'What is the trouble?'

'The foxes are chasing me.'

'Then what do you want?'

'To become a fox.'

'All right, become a fox.'

Then the fox came and said, 'Oh, now tigers are chasing me.'

'Then what do you want?'

'I want to become a tiger.'

'All right, become a tiger.'

Now the tiger began to stare at the saintly person. 'I shall eat you,' the tiger said.

'Oh, you shall eat me? I have made you a tiger, and you want to eat me!'

'Yes, I am a tiger, and now I shall eat you.'

Then the saintly person cursed him: 'Again become a rat!' And the tiger became a rat.

So, our human civilization is like this. The other day I was reading the *World Almanac.* It said that within the next hundred years people will be living underground – like rats. Scientific advancement has created the atomic bomb to kill men, and when it will be used people will have to go underground and become like rats. From tiger to rat. That is going to happen; it is nature's law.

Materialists, in material consciousness, are engaged in producing so many things in the name of economic development. They think that by advancing in satisfying the material needs of man they will be happy, but they forget that everything they have produced will be destroyed in due course of time. From history we can see that there were many powerful empires on the surface of the globe that were constructed with great pain and great perseverance, but in due course of time they have all been destroyed. Still, the foolish materialists cannot understand that they are simply wasting time in producing so-called material necessities, which are destined to be vanquished in due course of time. This waste of energy is due to the ignorance of the mass of people, who do not know that they are eternal and that they have an eternal engagement also. They do not know that this span of life in a particular type of body is but a flash in the eternal journey. Not knowing this fact, they take the small flash of their present life to be everything, and they waste time in improving economic conditions.

But there is so much stimulation in this world. How can we focus on the eternal when this world is so full of ways to enjoy?

The body is composed of senses, and the senses are always hungry after their objects. The eyes see a beautiful person and tell us, 'Oh, there is a beautiful girl, a beautiful boy. Let's go see.' The ears are telling us, 'Oh, there is very nice music. Let us go hear it.' The tongue is saying, 'Oh, there is a very nice restaurant with palatable dishes. Let us go.' In this way the senses are dragging us from one place to another, and because of this we are perplexed.

It is imperative that we learn how to control the senses. Kṛṣṇa indicates that one who identifies with the illusory material body cannot establish himself in his proper identity as spirit soul. We are all seeking enjoyment through these bodies, but bodily enjoyment is not our actual enjoyment. It is artificial. We have to understand that if we want to continue in this artificial enjoyment, we will not be able to attain our position of eternal enjoyment.

But isn't it natural to enjoy the senses?

A diseased man cannot enjoy life; his enjoyment of life is a false enjoyment. But when he is cured and healthy, then he is able to enjoy. Similarly, as long as we are in the material conception of life, we are not actually enjoying ourselves but are simply becoming more and more entangled in material nature. If a sick man is not supposed to eat, his eating unrestrictedly actually kills him. Similarly, the more we increase material enjoyment, the more we become entangled in this world, and the more difficult it becomes to get free from material entrapment.

Unrestricted sense enjoyment in this bodily condition is the path of ignorance and death. The living entities are not without spiritual senses; every living being in his original, spiritual form has all the senses, which are now materially manifested, being covered by the material body and mind. The activities of the material senses are perverted reflections of the activities of the original, spiritual senses. In his diseased condition, the spirit soul engages in material activities under the material covering. Real sense enjoyment is possible only when the disease of materialism is removed. In our pure spiritual form, free from all material contamination, real enjoyment of the senses is possible. A patient must regain his health before he can truly enjoy sense pleasure again. Thus the aim of human life should not be to enjoy perverted sense enjoyment but to cure the material disease. Aggravation of the material disease is no sign of knowledge but a sign of ignorance. For good health, a person should not increase his fever from 40 degrees to 42 degrees but should reduce his temperature to the normal 37. That should be the aim of human life.

Still, shouldn't we appreciate life's pleasures?

Once, a foolish man who had no experience of the taste of sugarcane was told by a friend to taste its sweetness. When the man inquired about sugarcane's appearance, the friend imperfectly informed him that sugarcane resembles a bamboo stick. The foolish man thus began trying to extract sugarcane juice from a bamboo stick, but naturally he was baffled in his attempt.

That is the position of the illusioned living being in his search for eternal happiness within the material world, which is not only full of miseries but also transient and flickering. In the *Bhagavad-gītā,* the material world is described as full of miseries. The ambition for happiness is good, but the attempt to derive it from inert matter by so-called scientific arrangements is an illusion. Befooled persons cannot understand this.

The atheistic, or godless, civilization is a huge affair of sense gratification, and everyone is now mad after money to keep up an empty show. Everyone is seeking money because that is the medium of exchange for sense-gratificatory objects. As long as there is even a slight tinge of madness for sense gratification, peace will remain far, far away.

But why does the desire for sense gratification feel so normal?

The bodily senses are merely coverings over the eternal, spiritual senses of the soul. Therefore even after detaching ourselves from the body's senses, we still have senses and sensual needs. We enjoy sweets because of their taste. Everyone is trying to enjoy some taste, and we want to enjoy sex because there is some taste there. Material tastes are different from spiritual tastes because they are tasted and quickly finished. Material tastes last only a few minutes. You may take a sweet, taste it and say, 'Oh, that is very nice,' but you have to taste another in order to continue the enjoyment, and so material taste is not unlimited. Real, spiritual taste is without end. Spiritual taste cannot be forgotten; it goes on increasing.

Where did this world come from?

It is natural that a philosophical mind wants to know about the origin of the creation. At night he sees the stars in the sky, and he naturally speculates about their inhabitants. Such inquiries are natural for man because man has a developed consciousness that is higher than that of the animals.

We can see that everything we see has a maker, a creator, and we can conclude that this great cosmic manifestation also has a creator. This is reasoning. But rascals speculate that in the beginning there was a big chunk of matter and an explosion or whatever that started the universe. But if there was an explosion, there must have been some explosive, and if there was an explosive, there must have been some worker to set it off. Otherwise, how did the chunk of matter explode? Through our reasoning we can perceive that everything has some creator or cause.

The creation itself is evidence of the consciousness of the Supreme. Everyone can appreciate the cosmic manifestation and how nicely it is working. The sun and moon rise exactly on time without deviating even one ten-thousandth of a second, and the seasons change in the same way, bringing with them fruits and flowers. In this way the entire cosmic manifestation is going on in a very orderly, systematic way. So unless there is some very clever intelligence who knows everything, how could all this have been created? Some people say that all this has come from nothing. What is this nonsense? Can such a creation come from nothing? Does this idea show very good reasoning?

But isn't nature the cause of matter?

Inert matter is undoubtedly energy with a potential to interact, but it has no initiative of its own. The material energy, or nature, is not independently active. In the *Bhagavad-gītā* (9.10) it is clearly stated that the material nature does not work independently: the material nature, which is one of the Supreme's energies, is working under His direction, 'producing all moving and nonmoving beings'. Under the rule of His material energies, 'this manifestation is created and annihilated again and again'. When a foolish man sees a machine, he may think that it is working automatically, but actually it is not – there is a driver, someone in control, although we sometimes cannot see the controller behind the machine due to our defective vision.

Superficially, material nature appears to be the cause of creation, maintenance and destruction, but material nature is set into motion for creation by the supreme conscious being, the Personality of Godhead. He is the background of all creation, maintenance and destruction, and this is confirmed in the *Bhagavad-gītā*.

Why did the Supreme Person create this world?

Providence desires only the good. The living entity is in this material world due to the improper utilization of his will. Because the living entity wants to enjoy this material world, God is so kind that He gives him facilities and directions. When a child wants to play in a certain way, he is guided by some nurse or servant hired by the parents. Our position is something like that. We have given up the company of God to come to this material world to enjoy ourselves. So God has allowed us to come here, saying, 'All right, enjoy this experience, and when you understand that this material enjoyment is ultimately frustrating, you can come back.' Thus the Supreme Lord is guiding the enjoyment of all living beings, especially human beings, so that they may again return home, back to Godhead. Nature is the agent acting under the instructions of God. If the living entity is overly addicted to misusing his freedom, he is punished. This punishment is a consequence of the living entity's desire. God does not want a human being to become a village hog, but when one develops such a mentality by eating anything and everything, God gives the facility by providing the body of a hog so that he can even eat stool. God is situated in everyone's heart and is noting the desires of the living entity from within. According to one's desires, God orders material nature to provide a particular body. In this way one continues transmigrating from body to body, in various species of life.

What is the difference between the material world and the spiritual world?

The material world is described as a tree whose roots are upward and branches are below. We have experience of a tree whose roots are upward: if one stands on the bank of a river or any reservoir of water, he can see that the trees reflected in the water are upside down. The branches go downward and the roots upward. Similarly, this material world is a reflection of the spiritual world. The material world is but a shadow of reality. In the shadow there is no reality or substantiality, but from the shadow we can understand that there are substance and reality. In the desert there is no water, but the mirage suggests that there is such a thing as water. In the material world there is no water, there is no happiness, but the real water of actual happiness is there in the spiritual world.

Who is God?

Who God is is explained in *Śrīmad-Bhāgavatam* (1.1.1). God is He from whom everything emanates. That is God – the Supreme Being from whom everything emanates. Now, what is the nature of that Supreme Being? Is He a dead stone or a living entity? That is also explained: the Supreme Being is fully cognizant of everything, directly and indirectly. Unless He is fully cognizant of everything, He cannot be God. And He is also fully independent.

How can a person be the cause of everything?

Science and philosophy mean finding out the ultimate cause of everything. And we get information from the Vedic literature that Kṛṣṇa is the cause of all causes. When I say 'Kṛṣṇa' I mean God. Just try to understand. I am caused by my father; my father is caused by his father, who is caused by his father, who is caused by his father. In this way, if you go on searching, you'll ultimately come to someone who is the cause who has no cause. The cause that has no cause is Kṛṣṇa. I may be the cause of my son, but at the same time I am the result of another cause (my father). But the Vedic literature says that Kṛṣṇa is the original person; He has no cause.

It is very difficult for a person who is too materially affected to understand the personal nature of the Supreme Absolute Truth. Generally, people who are attached to the bodily conception of life are so absorbed in materialism that it is almost impossible for them to understand how the Supreme can be a person. Such materialists cannot even imagine that there is a transcendental body which is imperishable, full of knowledge and eternally blissful.

Why should I put my faith in these ancient Vedic perspectives?

Actually, the process of belief and revelation is not foreign to us. Every day we place faith in something that we have confidence will be revealed later. We may purchase a ticket to go to India, and on the basis of the ticket we have faith that we will be transported there. Why should we pay money for a ticket? We do not just give the money to anyone. The company is authorized and the airline is authorized, so faith is created. Without faith we cannot take one step forward in the ordinary course of our life. Faith we must have, but it must be faith in that which is authorized. It is not that we have blind faith but that we accept something that is recognized. The *Bhagavad-gītā* is recognized and accepted as scripture by all classes of men in India, and as far as outside India is concerned, many scholars, theologians and philosophers accept the *Bhagavad-gītā* as a great, authoritative work. There is no question that the *Bhagavad-gītā* is an authority. Even Professor Albert Einstein, such a scientist, read the *Bhagavad-gītā* regularly.

3

The Lord of Attraction

Everyone has his or her own conception of God. Some think of Him as an old-man judge seated on a throne, rewarding those who follow His law and punishing those who don't. Others think of Him as an imaginary being who gives hope to those who can't handle the harsh realities of life. For some He is 'the opiate of the masses', and they use Him to manipulate others socially or politically. Some think of Him as either impotent to stop the suffering in the world or simply uninterested in it. Still others see Him as the cosmic order-supplier, a convenient port of call in times of need and want but of little other import.

The philosophy of bhakti-yoga, however, paints a different picture of God: not only does God exist, but He is the source of all attractiveness and pleasure. In fact, Kṛṣṇa, the name of God mentioned in the previous chapter, literally means 'the all-attractive one', He is the God of love, and from Him, the original seed of existence, comes the beautiful and glorious creation we see around us.

Can you tell me something about God?

Who is God? The person who possesses all the riches, all the strength, all the wisdom, all the beauty, all renunciation, like that – He is called Bhagavān, or the Supreme Person. So there is a definition.

Generally people say, 'God is great.' But they do not know how great He is. God's greatness is indicated perfectly by the name Kṛṣṇa. If you want a perfect definition of the word *God,* then it is Kṛṣṇa, because the word *kṛṣṇa* means 'all-attractive'. Unless one is all-attractive, how can He be God, the greatest? If one is great, he must be attractive.

For example, John D. Rockefeller and Henry Ford were considered great men because they were very rich. Their great wealth made them attractive. So wealth is one feature of attraction. Therefore God must be the wealthiest person. Beauty is another attractive feature, so God must be the most beautiful person. Many people, when they see a picture of Kṛṣṇa, are convinced they have never seen such a beautiful person, although He's a little blackish. Similarly, Kṛṣṇa fully possesses the attractive opulences of strength, wisdom, fame and renunciation. And because these six opulences of infinite wealth, beauty, strength, wisdom, fame and renunciation make Him all-attractive, God is known by the name Kṛṣṇa, 'all-attractive'. With these transcendental opulences He can attract the richest person, the most beautiful person, the strongest person, the wisest person, the most famous person and the most renounced person.

Don't you talk about Kṛṣṇa having lived on earth?

Kṛṣṇa, the Supreme Personality of Godhead, is a historical person who appeared on this earth five thousand years ago. He stayed on this earth for 125 years and played exactly like a human being, but His activities were unparalleled. From the very moment of His appearance to the moment of His disappearance, every one of His activities is unparalleled in the history of the world, and therefore anyone who knows what we mean by Godhead will accept Kṛṣṇa as the Supreme Personality of Godhead. No one is equal to the Godhead, and no one is greater than Him. That is the import of the familiar saying 'God is great.'

But doesn't Kṛṣṇa also live in heaven or a spiritual world?

The *Īśopaniṣad* states, 'The Supreme Lord walks and does not walk. He is far away, but He is very near as well. He is within everything, and yet He is outside of everything.' How can Kṛṣṇa walk and also not walk? As a crude example, consider how the sun at noontime shines on your head. If you begin walking, you will see that the sun is accompanying you. About forty years ago, when I was a married man, I was walking with my second son in the evening. He was four years old. All of a sudden he said, 'Father, why is the moon following us?' You see? The moon and the sun are fixed in the sky, yet they seem to be moving with us. Similarly, if you are going on an airplane or train, you will see that the moon or sun is going with you. If this is possible for the sun and the moon, why can't Kṛṣṇa also walk with you? 'Although He is situated far away, He is very near as well.' In other words, although Kṛṣṇa is in Goloka Vṛndāvana, the spiritual world, enjoying pastimes with His associates, He is simultaneously everywhere in this material world.

Doesn't this require faith?

For those who are hesitant and have no faith, Kṛṣṇa consciousness is very difficult. Even in our daily affairs a certain amount of faith is required. When we buy a ticket, we have faith that the airline company will take us to our destination. Without faith we cannot even live in the material world, what to speak of making spiritual progress. Where are we to keep our faith? In the authority. We should not book our ticket with an unauthorized company. Faith must be in Kṛṣṇa, the speaker of the *Bhagavad-gītā.*

Isn't it limiting or childish to depict God with a humanlike form?

Actually, God has a form. Why not? The *Vedānta-sūtra* (1.1.1) says, 'The Supreme Absolute Truth is that from whom or from which everything emanates.' Now, we have forms. And not only us, but all the different kinds of living entities have forms. Where have those forms come from? From where have these forms originated? These are very common-sense questions. If God is not a person, then how have His sons become persons? If my father is not a person, how have I become a person? If my father has no form, where did I get my form from? Nonetheless, when people are frustrated, when they see that their bodily forms are troublesome, they develop an opposite conception of form, and they imagine that God must be formless. But the *Brahma-saṁhitā* says no. God has a form, but His form is eternal and full of knowledge and bliss. So God has a form, but His form is full of pleasure, full of knowledge and eternal.

Now, let's compare our body to God's. Our body is neither eternal nor full of pleasure nor full of knowledge. So our form is clearly different from God's. But as soon as we think of form, we think the form must be like ours. Therefore we think that since God must be the opposite of us, He must have no form.

Have you seen God?

Yes, I am seeing God. You can also see God. Everyone can see God. But you must have the qualification. Suppose something is wrong with a motorcar and it is not running. Everyone is seeing it, but a mechanic sees it differently. He's qualified to see it with greater understanding. So he replaces some missing part and immediately the car runs. Although to see a machine we require so much qualification, we want to see God without any qualification. Just see the folly!

Those who are filled with love of God see God constantly before them. It is not that we saw God last night and He is no longer present. No. For one who is Kṛṣṇa conscious, Kṛṣṇa is always present and can be perceived constantly. We simply have to develop the eyes to see Him.

How can I qualify myself to see God?

With your present blunt material senses you cannot immediately perceive God's spiritual form, name, qualities, pastimes and paraphernalia. And because people in the present civilization have no power to understand God, nor are they guided by some person who can help them understand God, they have become godless. But if you read Vedic scriptures like the *Īśopaniṣad* and *Bhagavad-gītā* under superior guidance and follow the rules and regulations, eventually God will be revealed to you. You cannot see God or understand God by your own endeavour. You have to surrender to the process by which God can be known. Then He will reveal Himself. He is the supreme controller; you are being controlled. So how can you control God? 'O God, come here. I want to see You.' God is not so cheap that by your order He will come and be seen by you. No, that is not possible. You must always remember, 'God is the supreme controller and I am controlled. So if I can please God by my service, then He will reveal Himself to me.' That is the process of knowing God.

I'm not really into religion – it causes so much divisiveness and conflict.

How to love God: this is the one religion. Will the Christians say, 'No, we don't want to love God'? Will the Muslims say, 'No, no, we don't want to love God'? Religion means how to love God, and any religion that teaches how to love God – that is perfect. It doesn't matter whether you are Christian or Muslim or Hindu. *Śrīmad-Bhāgavatam* (6.3.19) says, 'Real religion is directly enunciated by Bhagavān, the Supreme Personality of Godhead.' So, Bhagavān, Lord Kṛṣṇa, says 'surrender to Me'. Of course, you cannot surrender until you love. When one loves God – when one reaches the platform where he thinks, 'O Lord, I love You; I can sacrifice everything for You', that is the basic principle of religion. Therefore, that religion is perfect that teaches its followers how to love God. So let everyone come to this platform of loving God. That is Kṛṣṇa consciousness. We are teaching nothing but how to love God, how to sacrifice everything for God. That is real religion. Otherwise, it is all a bogus waste of time, simply a following of ritualistic ceremonies. That is not religion. That is superfluous.

When you're actually on the platform of love of God, you understand your relationship with God: 'I am part and parcel of God – and this dog is also part and parcel of God. And so is every other living entity.' Then you'll also extend your love to the animals. If you actually love God, then your love for insects is also there, because you understand, 'This insect has a different kind of body, but he is also part and parcel of God – he is my brother.' The *Bhagavad-gītā* (18.54) says you'll look on all living beings equally. Then you cannot maintain slaughterhouses. If you maintain slaughterhouses and disobey the order of Christ in the Bible – 'Thou shall not kill' – and you proclaim yourself a Christian, your so-called religion is simply a waste of time. Your going to the church and everything is simply a waste of time, because you have no love for God. That foolishness is going on all over the world. People are stamping themselves with some sectarian label, but there is no real religion.

How do I begin to love God?

Material consciousness has two psychic divisions. One is that I am the creator and the other is that I am the enjoyer. But actually the Supreme Lord is both the creator and the enjoyer, and the living entity, being part and parcel of the Supreme Lord, is neither the creator nor the enjoyer but a cooperator. He is the created and the enjoyed. For instance, a part of a machine cooperates with the whole machine; a part of the body cooperates with the whole body. The hands, legs, eyes and so on are all parts of the body, but they are not actually the enjoyers. The stomach is the enjoyer. The legs move, the hands supply food, the teeth chew, and all parts of the body are engaged in satisfying the stomach because the stomach is the principal factor that nourishes the body's organization. Therefore everything is given to the stomach. One nourishes the tree by watering its root, and one nourishes the body by feeding the stomach, for if the body is to be kept in a healthy state, then the parts of the body must cooperate to feed the stomach. Similarly, the Supreme Lord is the enjoyer and the creator, and we, as subordinate living beings, are meant to cooperate to satisfy Him. This cooperation will actually help us, just as food taken by the stomach will help all other parts of the body.

How does this love develop further?

The symptoms of love are described in the *Upadeśāmṛta* (4): If you love somebody, you must give him something and you must accept something from him. You must disclose your mind to him and he should disclose his mind to you. And you should give him some eatables, and whatever eatable thing he offers you, you accept. These six kinds of exchange develop love.

But if you do not even know the person, then where is the question of love? Suppose you love some boy or girl, then you will give some present, and he or she will give you some present – that develops love. You give something to eat, and whatever he or she gives you to eat, you eat. You disclose your mind: 'My dear such-and-such, I love you. This is my ambition.' And he or she makes some disclosure. These are the exchanges of love. But if there is no person-to-person meeting, where is the question of love? If I claim to love somebody, but I visit his house only once a week and ask, 'Please give me such-and-such', where is the exchange of love? Love means there is some exchange. If you love somebody but you have not given anything to that person or taken anything from him, where is the love?

The conclusion is, religion means to love God, and that means you must know who God is. There is no alternative. You must know the person who is God. Then you can have loving exchanges with Him.

Then how do I learn who God is?

The *Bhagavad-gītā* is the preliminary science of how to know God. If you want to know more, then read *Śrīmad-Bhāgavatam.* And if you are in intense love with God, read *Caitanya-caritāmṛta* – how your love for God can be still more intensified. So the *Bhagavad-gītā* is the preliminary book to understand God and surrender. And from the surrendering point, further progress – that is *Śrīmad-Bhāgavatam.* And when the love is intense, to make it more intensified – that is *Caitanya-caritāmṛta.* Śrī Caitanya Mahāprabhu was mad after God. He cried, 'I find everything vacant without Kṛṣṇa.' That is the supreme ecstasy.

So understand God and learn how to love Him and your life will be perfect. What is your process of loving God? If you do not know your relationship with God and others' relationship with God, then how can you love God? If you have no understanding of what God is, where is the question of love? Love is not mere fantasy or imagination. You cannot love air. You love a person, a beautiful person. If you merely say, 'I love the air, I love the sky', what question is there of love? There must be a person. So who is that person we want to love?

Unfortunately, most people have no personal conception of

God. Nor can they describe the Lord's personal beauty, knowledge, strength – His fullness in the six personal opulences. There is no such description. They have some conception of God, but actually they do not know what God is.

What do you think about people who claim to be God?

In the *Īśopaniṣad,* the word *īśa* is used to describe the Supreme Personality of Godhead. *Īśa* means 'controller'. Do you think you are controlled or not? Is there any person anywhere within this universe who is not controlled? Can anyone say, 'I am not controlled'? Nobody can say that. So if you are controlled, then why do you declare, 'I am not controlled, I am independent, I am God'? Why this nonsense? Impersonalists claim, 'I am God, you are God, everyone is God.' But if they are controlled, how can they be God? Does this make any sense? God is never controlled; He is the supreme controller. So if somebody is controlled, immediately we should know that he is not God.

Of course, some rascals claim that they are not controlled. I know one such rascal who has a society and is preaching, 'I am God'. But one day I saw him with a toothache; he was moaning, 'Ohhh!' So I asked him, 'You claim that you are God, the supreme controller, but now you are under the control of a toothache. What kind of God are you?' If you see someone who claims that he is God or that everyone is God, you should immediately know such a person is a number-one rascal.

What does it mean to be conscious of Kṛṣṇa?

A person in Kṛṣṇa consciousness certainly sees Lord Kṛṣṇa everywhere, and he sees everything in Kṛṣṇa. Such a person may appear to see all separate manifestations of the material nature, but in each and every instance he is conscious of Kṛṣṇa, knowing that everything is the manifestation of Kṛṣṇa's energy. Nothing can exist without Kṛṣṇa, and Kṛṣṇa is the Lord of everything – this is the basic principle of Kṛṣṇa consciousness.

Your Kṛṣṇa consciousness is already there; I am simply helping you to revive it. Just like a boy or a girl, when they are grown up, it is not that anybody has instructed them how to enjoy sex life. It is already there, but it was not experienced when they were children. But with the grown-up age the propensities automatically become manifest. Nobody has to learn these things. Similarly, Kṛṣṇa consciousness is not a thing to be learned. It is to be revived. Just like the matches. There is already fire. If you simply rub the stick, the fire will come.

How can I think of God in my daily life?

If you have not developed Kṛṣṇa consciousness to the degree that you can always see God in your heart, then you can see Him in the material world, as prescribed in the scriptures. For example, in the *Bhagavad-gītā* (7.8) Kṛṣṇa says, 'I am the taste of water.' So, you can see Kṛṣṇa while drinking water if you remember, 'The taste of this water is Kṛṣṇa.' Is it very difficult? Not at all. Then Kṛṣṇa says, 'I am the light of the sun and the moon.' If while drinking water you forget that Kṛṣṇa is the taste, you can see Him by remembering that He is the light of the sun and the moon. So when people ask, 'Have you seen God?' we reply, 'Yes, and you have also seen Him, because Kṛṣṇa says, "I am the sunshine".' Who has not seen sunshine? You have to begin seeing God in this way – by remembering Him when you taste water, when you see sunshine, and so on. Such remembrance of God is also seeing Him. Spiritual seeing is not done simply with the eyes. Because Kṛṣṇa is absolute, you can also see Him by chanting His name or by describing Him. When you hear of Kṛṣṇa, you are seeing Kṛṣṇa; when you chant about Kṛṣṇa, you are seeing Kṛṣṇa; when you think of Kṛṣṇa, you are seeing Kṛṣṇa. This is the process for seeing God.

How will this help the world?

We have failed to create peace and harmony in human society, even by such great attempts as the United Nations, because we do not know the right method. The method is very simple, but one has to understand it with a cool head. If we learn the simple and natural process of loving Kṛṣṇa, then it is very easy to immediately and simultaneously love every living being. It is like pouring water on the root of a tree or supplying food to one's stomach. The method of pouring water on the root of a tree or supplying food to the stomach is universally scientific and practical, as every one of us has experienced. Everyone knows well that when we eat something or, in other words, when we put food in the stomach, the energy created by such action is immediately distributed throughout the whole body. Similarly, when we pour water on the root, the energy thus created is immediately distributed throughout the entirety of even the largest tree. It is not possible to water the tree part by part, nor is it possible to feed the different parts of the body separately. We have to learn how to turn the one switch that will immediately brighten everything, everywhere. One who does not know this method is missing the point of life.

So the real peace formula is that one must know that God is the proprietor of this entire universe, including the United States of America. He is the proprietor of Russia, He is the proprietor of China, He is the proprietor of India – of everything. But because we claim that *we* are the proprietors, there is fighting, there is discord, there is disagreement, and how can there be peace?

First of all, one has to accept that God is the proprietor of everything. We are simply guests for fifty or a hundred years. We come and go, and while one is here, he is absorbed in this thought: 'This is my land. This is my family. This is my body. This is my property.' And when there is an order from the Supreme for one to leave his home, his property, his body, his family, his money, his bank balance, and it is all gone, one has to take another place.

Actually, this is ignorance. Peace can be had when one understands that God is the proprietor of everything. One's friends, mother, grandfather and the president are all guests of time. When this knowledge is accepted, then there will be peace.

We are searching for a friend to give us peace and tranquillity. That friend is Kṛṣṇa, God. Just make friendship with Him; you'll find everyone to be your friend. Because God is situated in everyone's heart, if you make friendship with God, He will dictate from within so that you will also be treated in a friendly way. If you make friendship with the police commissioner, you receive some advantage. If you make friendship with the president, everyone will be your friend because everyone is under the president. If you want something from any officer, simply call the president, and he will say, 'All right, look after this man.' Everything is taken care of. Just try to have friendship with God, and everyone will be your friend. If all people understand this very nice fact, that God is everyone's friend and that He is the supreme proprietor, they will become peaceful.

4

The Love Vacuum

Theologian Thomas Merton said, 'Love is our true destiny. We do not find the meaning of life by ourselves alone – we find it with another.' It's natural to want to love and be loved. So most of us spend our lives looking for those persons and objects in which we can repose our love and have it reciprocated – perhaps a spouse or family or country or pet. But although we're made for love, most people seem unfulfilled or disappointed in their attempts to find it. Why do people live happily ever after in the movies but rarely in real life?

Like the search for pleasure, the search for love has to begin with making a spiritual connection with the self and then with the source of love. When you water the root of a tree, you automatically water the trunk, branches, twigs and leaves. In the same way, when you water the root of your need to love and be loved by reposing your love in the source of all love, Kṛṣṇa, you flourish. Not only do you reconnect with yourself but you can become a conduit of love for others.

How can I find true love?

The basic principle of the living condition is that we have a general propensity to love someone. No one can live without loving someone else. This propensity is present in every living being. Even an animal like a tiger has this loving propensity at least in a dormant stage, and it is certainly present in the human beings. The missing point, however, is where to repose our love so that everyone can become happy. At the present moment the human society teaches one to love his country or family or his personal self, but there is no information where to repose the loving propensity so that everyone can become happy. That missing point is Kṛṣṇa.

In the primary stage a child loves his parents, then his brothers and sisters and, as he daily grows up, he begins to love his family, society, community, country, nation or even the whole human society. But the loving propensity is not satisfied even by loving all human society; that loving propensity remains imperfectly fulfilled until we know who is the supreme beloved. Our love can be fully satisfied only when it is reposed in Kṛṣṇa.

But what about loving my spouse? Can't we find love in the relationships we have in this world?

Kṛṣṇa is related to everyone as eternal father, and consequently when we establish a Kṛṣṇa conscious relationship, we become related to everyone. When one marries, he automatically establishes a relationship with the spouse's family. Similarly, if we reestablish our original relationship with Kṛṣṇa, we will establish our true relationship with everyone else. That is the ground for real universal love. Universal love is artificial and cannot endure unless we establish our relationship with the centre. One is American if he is born in America, and thus other Americans become members of his family, but if he is born elsewhere, he has no relationship with Americans. On the mundane platform all relationships are relative. Our relationship with Kṛṣṇa, however, is eternal and not subject to time and circumstance.

Unfortunately, we have forgotten that Kṛṣṇa, God, is all-pervading. This memory has to be revived. As soon as we revive our Kṛṣṇa consciousness, we can see everything in relationship with Kṛṣṇa, and then everything becomes lovable. Now I love you or you love me, but that love is on the platform of this ephemeral body. But when love of Kṛṣṇa is developed, I will love not only you but every living entity because the outward designation, the body, will be forgotten. When a person becomes fully Kṛṣṇa conscious, he does not think, 'Here is a man, here is an animal, here is a cat, here is a dog, here is a worm.' He sees everyone as part and parcel of Kṛṣṇa. This is very nicely explained in the *Bhagavad-gītā:* 'One who is actually learned in Kṛṣṇa consciousness becomes a lover of everyone in the universe.'

I've been told that universal love is only possible when we become one with God.

Our process is to dovetail our consciousness with Kṛṣṇa consciousness – that will make us perfect. It is not that we merge into that consciousness. In one sense we 'merge', but still we keep our individuality. That is the difference between impersonalist philosophy and Kṛṣṇa conscious philosophy. The impersonalist philosopher says that perfection means to merge into the Supreme and lose our individuality. We say that in the perfectional stage we merge into the Supreme but keep our individuality. How is that? An airplane starts from the airport and climbs up and up, and when it goes very high we cannot see it: we can simply see sky. But the airplane is not lost – it is still there. Another example is that of a green bird entering into a big green tree. We cannot distinguish the bird from the tree, but they both continue to exist. Similarly, the supreme consciousness is Kṛṣṇa, and when we dovetail our individual consciousness with the Supreme, we become perfect –

but keep our individuality. Every individual person, every individual being, maintains his individuality eternally, even when dovetailed with the Supreme.

What does it mean to have a relationship with God?

We must understand the meaning of relationships with Kṛṣṇa. In this material world we have many relationships as father or mother, husband or wife. Whatever relationships we find here are but a perverted reflection of the relationships we have with the Supreme Lord. Whatever we find in this material world is born of the Absolute Truth, but here it is pervertedly reflected in time. Whatever relationship we have with Kṛṣṇa goes on. If we have a relationship in friendship, that friendship is eternal and continues from life to life. In the material world, a friendship exists for a few years and then breaks; therefore it is called perverted, temporal or unreal. If we make our friendship with Kṛṣṇa, it will never break. If we make our master Kṛṣṇa, we will never be cheated. If we love Kṛṣṇa as our son, He will never die. If we love Kṛṣṇa as our lover, He will be the best of all and there will be no separation. And because Kṛṣṇa is the Supreme Lord, He is unlimited and has an unlimited number of devotees.

Should I see God as my eternal father?

Once they understand their relationship with God, people generally believe that God is the father, and the son's business is to ask the father for whatever he needs. But that is really a lesser relationship. If you understand God perfectly, then there are intimate relationships also. Your intimate relationship will be revealed when you are perfectly liberated. Each and every living creature has a particular relationship with God, but we have, for now, forgotten it. When that relationship is revealed in the process of devotional activities, or Kṛṣṇa consciousness, you will know that that is the perfection of your life. Kṛṣṇa consciousness is a great science; it is not a sentimental speculation regarding love. It is based on scientific propositions described in the *Bhagavad-gītā.*

Can I have a deep, loving relationship with God?

You may want Kṛṣṇa as your lover or as your son; you may want Kṛṣṇa as your friend or as your master. You may want Kṛṣṇa as the Supreme Sublime. These five different kinds of direct relationships with Kṛṣṇa are called devotion, or bhakti. They entail no material profit.

The concept of accepting God as a son is superior to the concept of accepting God as a father. There is a distinction. The relationship between father and son is that the son wants to take something from the father. The father's relationship with the son is that the father always wants to give something to the son. Therefore the relationship with God, or Kṛṣṇa, as son is better than the relationship with Kṛṣṇa by one who thinks, 'If I accept God as my father, then my business will be to ask for my necessities from Him.' But if I become the father of Kṛṣṇa, then from the very beginning of His childhood my business will be to serve Him.

This concept is sublime. Kṛṣṇa's mother, Yaśodā, is thinking, 'If I do not feed Kṛṣṇa sumptuously, He will die.' She forgets that Kṛṣṇa is the Supreme Lord, that He is sustaining the three worlds. She forgets that only one Lord is supplying the necessities of all the living entities. This same Personality of Godhead has become the son of Yaśodā, and she is thinking, 'If I do not feed Him nicely, He will die.' This is love. She has forgotten that it is the Supreme Personality of Godhead who has appeared before her as a little child.

This relationship of attachment is very sublime. It requires time to understand, but there is a position where, instead of asking, 'O God, please give us our daily bread', you can instead think that God will die if you do not supply bread to Him. This is the ecstasy of extreme love. There is such a relationship between Kṛṣṇa and His devotee Rādhārāṇī, the greatest devotee, the greatest lover of Kṛṣṇa. Mother Yaśodā is His lover as a parent; Sudāmā is His lover as a friend; Arjuna also as a friend – there are millions and billions of different kinds of direct devotees of Kṛṣṇa.

Why does God appear in this world?

The father is always affectionate to the son. The son may forget the father, but the father can never forget the son. Kṛṣṇa comes to the material universe, out of His love for us, in order to deliver us from the miseries of birth and death. He says, 'My dear sons, why are you rotting in this miserable world? Come to Me, and I'll give you all protection.' We are sons of the Supreme, and we can enjoy life very supremely, without any misery and without any doubt. Therefore we should not think that Kṛṣṇa comes here just as we do, being obliged by the laws of nature. The Sanskrit word *avatāra* literally means 'he who descends'. One who descends from the spiritual universe into the material universe by his own will is called an *avatāra.* Sometimes Kṛṣṇa descends Himself, and sometimes He sends His representative.

Kṛṣṇa's appearance and disappearance are meant to put an end to the living entities' transmigration from one body to another, and therefore one should understand the greatness of the plan behind Kṛṣṇa's appearance and disappearance. It is not that Kṛṣṇa comes whimsically. He has a great plan; otherwise why should He come here? He is very much eager to take us back home, back to Godhead. That is Kṛṣṇa's business.

When did God last appear?

The *avatāra* for this age, Lord Caitanya, is described in the Vedic literature. We cannot accept anyone as an *avatāra* unless he has the symptoms described in the scriptures. We do not whimsically accept Lord Caitanya as an *avatāra* on the basis of votes. Nowadays it has become a fashion that any man can come and say that he is God or an incarnation of God, and some fools and rascals will accept it: 'Oh, he is God.' We do not accept an *avatāra* like that. We take evidence from the *Vedas*. An *avatāra* must conform to descriptions in the *Vedas*. Then we accept Him; otherwise no. For each *avatāra* there is a description in the *Vedas:* He will appear at such and such a place, in such and such a form, and He will act like this. That is the nature of Vedic evidence.

Although Kṛṣṇa gave us this message of the *Bhagavad-gītā* so that we could understand Him, many people missed the opportunity. Therefore Kṛṣṇa, out of His compassion, came again, as a devotee, and showed us how to surrender to Kṛṣṇa.

Caitanya Mahāprabhu is Kṛṣṇa Himself, and He is teaching how to develop love of God by a very simple method. He says simply to chant Hare Kṛṣṇa: 'In this age, simply go on chanting the Hare Kṛṣṇa mantra. There is no other alternative.' People are embarrassed by so many methods of realization. They cannot take to the actual ritualistic processes of meditation or yoga; it is not possible. Therefore Lord Caitanya says that if one takes up this process of chanting, then immediately he can reach the platform of realization.

The chanting process offered by Lord Caitanya for achieving love of God is called *saṅkīrtana. Saṅkīrtana* is a Sanskrit word. *Sam* means *samyak,* 'complete', and *kīrtana* means 'glorifying' or 'describing'. So a complete description of the Lord means a complete glorification of the Supreme, or the Supreme Complete Whole.

Why are you so convinced that Kṛṣṇa exists?

If one becomes advanced in Kṛṣṇa consciousness he will realize God directly. For example, through realization I am firmly convinced of whatever I am saying here about Kṛṣṇa. I am not speaking blindly. Similarly, anyone can realize God. Direct knowledge of God will be revealed to anyone who sticks to the process of Kṛṣṇa consciousness. Such a person will actually understand, 'Yes, there is a spiritual kingdom where God resides, and I have to go there. I must prepare to go there.' Before going to another country, one may hear so much about it, but when he actually goes there he understands everything directly. Similarly, if one takes up the process of Kṛṣṇa consciousness, one day he'll understand God and the kingdom of God directly, and the whole problem of his life will be solved.

How do you remain conscious of Kṛṣṇa at all times?

As soon as you see the sunshine, you can immediately think of the sun. Is that not so? In the morning, as soon as you see the sunshine shining in your window, you can immediately remember the sun. You are confident the sun is there, because you know that without the sun there cannot be any sunshine. Similarly, whenever we see something, we should immediately think of Kṛṣṇa with reference to that particular thing because that thing is a manifestation of Kṛṣṇa's energy. And because the energy is not different from the energetic, those who have understood Kṛṣṇa along with His energies do not see anything except Kṛṣṇa. Therefore for them there is no material world. To a perfect devotee, everything is spiritual.

Can I pray to God for help?

People ordinarily go to Kṛṣṇa to maintain their attachment to this material world. 'O God', they pray, 'give us our daily bread.' They have attachment to this material world, and to live in this material world they pray for supplies of material things so that they can maintain their status quo. This is called material attachment. Although in one sense, of course, it is good that people go to God to secure their material position, that is not actually desirable. Rather than worship God to increase one's opulence in the material world, one should become free from material attachment. For bhakti-yoga, or Kṛṣṇa consciousness, therefore, we should be detached.

Then what kind of prayer should we offer?

True religion teaches causeless love of God. It does not say, 'I love God because He supplies me nice objects for my sense gratification.' That is not love. God is great, God is our eternal father, and it is our duty to love Him. There is no question of barter or exchange. We should not think, 'Oh, God gives me my daily bread; therefore I love God.' God gives daily bread even to the cats and dogs. Since He is the father of everyone, He is supplying everyone food. So loving God for daily bread is not love. Love is without reason. Even if God does not supply us our daily bread, we should love Him. That is true love. As Caitanya Mahāprabhu said, 'I know no one but Kṛṣṇa as my Lord, and He shall remain so even if He handles me roughly by His embrace or makes me broken-hearted by not being present before me. He is completely free to do anything and everything, for He is always my worshipful Lord, unconditionally.' That is the sentiment of one who is established in pure love of God. When we attain that stage of love of God, we will find that everything is full of pleasure; God is full of pleasure, and we also are full of pleasure.

Our only prayer should be that the Lord enable us to serve Him birth after birth. Our prayer should be, 'Dear Lord, You are so great that I want to engage in Your service. I have been serving all these rascals, and I am not satisfied. Now I have come to You, please engage me in Your service.' This is the last word in prayer.

5

Honest Religion Defined

Many people these days prefer to call themselves 'spiritual' rather than 'religious'. They feel that 'spirituality' transcends dogma, institutions, ritual and sectarian boundaries, whereas religion is archaic and divisive, creating an overblown sense of 'us and them'.

But bhakti-yoga doesn't distinguish much between these two terms. The focus of bhakti is, as Śrīmad-Bhāgavatam (1.1.2) defines, pursuit of the highest truth without any material motivation. In the same text the Bhāgavatam defines the highest truth as 'reality distinguished from illusion for the welfare of all'. This truth uproots suffering – in ourselves and in those we share it with. Śrīmad-Bhāgavatam (1.2.10) also defines the purpose of human life: 'Life's desires should never be directed towards sense gratification. One should desire only a healthy life, or self-preservation, since a human being is meant for inquiry about the Absolute Truth. Nothing else should be the goal of one's works.'

What is religion?

Real religion means to know God, our relation with Him and our duties in relation with Him, and to know ultimately our destination after leaving this material body. The conditioned souls, who are entrapped by the material energy, hardly know all these principles of life.

Why do we need religion?

All scriptures, all religious principles, are meant to elevate man from the animal platform to the human platform. Therefore a person without religious principles, without God consciousness, is no better than an animal. That is the verdict of the Vedic literature: eating, sleeping, sex and defence – these four principles are common to both human beings and animals. The distinction between human life and animal life is that a man can search after God but an animal cannot. That is the difference. Therefore a man without that urge for searching after God is no better than an animal.

One may learn about his relationship with God by any process – through Christianity, the Vedic literature or the Koran – but it must be learned. The purpose of this Kṛṣṇa consciousness movement is not to make Christians into Hindus or Hindus into Christians but to inform everyone that the duty of a human being is to understand his relationship with God. One must learn this; otherwise he is simply wasting his time by engaging in animalistic propensities. We must all try to love Kṛṣṇa, or God. If one has a process, he should practise it, or he can come and learn this process.

Why are there different religions in the world?

The major religions of the world – Christianity, Hinduism, Buddhism and Islam – believe in some supreme authority or personality coming down from the kingdom of God. In the Christian religion, Jesus Christ claimed to be the son of God and to be coming from the kingdom of God to reclaim conditioned souls. As followers of the *Bhagavad-gītā,* we admit this claim to be true. So basically there is no difference of opinion. In details there may be differences due to differences in culture, climate and people, but the basic principle remains the same – that is, God or His representatives come to reclaim conditioned souls.

How do I decide what spiritual process to follow?

If one is serious about understanding love of God, he should consider which process is practical. One should not think, 'Why should I follow Hindu, or Vedic, scriptures?' The purpose of following the Vedic scriptures is to develop love of God. When students come to America for a higher education, they do not consider the fact that the teachers may be American, German or of other nationalities. If one wants a higher education, he simply comes and takes it. Similarly, if there is an effective process for understanding and approaching God, like this Kṛṣṇa consciousness process, one should take it.

What's the essence of religion?

In English dictionaries the word *dharma* is generally translated as 'religion', a kind of faith, but the actual meaning of dharma is 'essential characteristic'. For example, sugar's dharma, or essential characteristic, is sweetness. If you are given some white powder and you find that it is not sweet, you will at once say, 'Oh, this is not sugar; it is something else.' So sweetness is the dharma of sugar. Similarly, a salty taste is the dharma of salt, and pungency is the dharma of chilli. What is your essential characteristic? You are a living entity, and you have to understand your essential characteristic. That characteristic is your dharma, or religion – not the Christian or Hindu religion, this or that religion. Your eternal, essential characteristic – that is your religion.

And what is that characteristic? Your essential characteristic is that you want to love somebody, and therefore you want to serve him. That is your essential characteristic. You love your family, you love your society, you love your community, you love your country. And because you love them, you want to serve them. That tendency to engage in loving service is your essential characteristic, your dharma. Whether you are a Christian, a Muslim or a Hindu, this characteristic will remain. Suppose today you are a Christian. Tomorrow you may become a Hindu, but your serving mood, that loving spirit, will stay with you. Therefore the tendency to love and serve others is your dharma, or your religion. This is the universal form of religion.

You have to apply your loving service in such a way that you will be completely satisfied. Because your loving spirit is now misplaced, you are not happy. You are frustrated and confused. The *Śrīmad-Bhāgavatam* (1.2.6) tells us how to apply our spirit of loving devotion perfectly: that religion is first class which trains you to love God. And by this religion you will become completely satisfied.

What is the perfection of spiritual practice?

Religion does not mean that you go to a temple, mosque or church and as a matter of formality observe some rituals, make some donation and then come back home and do all kinds of nonsense. That is not religion.

It doesn't matter whether you follow the Hindu, Muslim or Christian religion: if you are developing love of God, then you are perfect in your religion. And what kind of love should we develop for God? It must be without any selfish motivation – 'O Lord, I love you because You supply me so many nice things. You are my order supplier.' No, we should not have this sort of love for God. It should not depend on any exchange.

Caitanya Mahāprabhu taught, 'O Lord! Whether You trample me under Your feet or embrace me or leave me broken-hearted by not being present before me, that does not matter. You are completely free to do anything, for You are my worshipable Lord unconditionally.' That is love. We should think, 'God may do whatever He likes, yet I will still love Him. I don't want anything in exchange.' That is the sort of love Kṛṣṇa wants. It is not that God wants you to love Him for His benefit. It is for your benefit. If you do otherwise, you will never be happy.

But you seem to follow a particular religion. Do you think your religion is the best?

No. The *Śrīmad-Bhāgavatam* does not mention that the Hindu religion is first class or the Christian religion is first class or the Muslim religion is first class or some other religion is first class. *Śrīmad-Bhāgavatam* says that that religion is first class which helps one advance his devotional service and love of God. That's all. This is the definition of a first-class religion. We do not analyse that one religion is first class or that another religion is last class. Of course, there are three qualities in the material world (goodness, passion and ignorance), and religious conceptions are created according to these qualities. But the purpose of religion is to understand God and to learn how to love God. Any religious system, if it teaches one how to love God, is first class. Otherwise, it is useless. One may prosecute his religious principles very rigidly and very nicely, but if his love of God is nil, if his love of matter is simply enhanced, then his religion is no religion.

The word *veda* means 'book of knowledge'. There are many books of knowledge, and they vary according to the country, population, environment, etc. In India the books of knowledge are referred to as the *Vedas*. In the West they are called the Old

Testament and New Testament. The Muslims accept the Koran. What is the purpose of all these books of knowledge? They are to train us to understand our position as pure soul. Their purpose is to restrict bodily activities by certain rules and regulations, and these rules and regulations are known as codes of morality. The Bible, for instance, has ten commandments intended to regulate our lives. The body must be controlled in order for us to reach the highest perfection, and without regulative principles, it is not possible to perfect our lives. The regulative principles may differ from country to country or from scripture to scripture, but that doesn't matter, for they are made according to the time and circumstance and the mentality of the people. But the principle of regulated control is the same. Similarly, the government sets down certain regulations to be obeyed by its citizens. There is no possibility of making advancement in government or civilization without some regulations.

Why aren't more people practising Kṛṣṇa consciousness?

Out of many millions of people, there may be only one who is interested in spiritual life. Generally, people are interested in eating, sleeping, mating and defending. So how can we expect to find many followers? It is not difficult to notice that people have lost their spiritual interest. And almost all those who are actually interested are being cheated by so-called spiritualists. You cannot judge simply by the number of followers. It is not a question of quantity but quality. My spiritual master used to say that if you take a langra mango, which is a first-class, topmost-quality mango in India, very costly, very sweet and very tasteful, and go door to door in order to distribute it for free, people will doubt: 'Why has this man brought this langra mango? Why is he trying to distribute it for free? There must be some motive behind it.' Similarly, Lord Caitanya distributed this Kṛṣṇa consciousness langra mango very cheaply, but people are so foolish that they think, 'Oh, they are simply chanting Hare Kṛṣṇa; what is there to it? This is meant for the foolish, who cannot speculate and do not have any higher standard of knowledge.' But that is not so. It is said: 'Out of millions and millions of people, only a few are interested in Kṛṣṇa consciousness.' Lord Caitanya said that innumerable living entities are wandering and transmigrating in the 8,400,000 species of life, one after another. Out of so many, one may come who is fortunate, who has spiritual fortune.

6

Yoga 101

If you'd like to know more about bhakti-yoga, the next few chapters will discuss it in more detail. As Śrīla Prabhupāda stated, bhakti-yoga, or Kṛṣṇa consciousness, is not a 'religion' but a path to recognizing your dharma and loving God which we can learn to follow whatever our faith.

Yoga is more than just physical postures practised for health and fitness. The word yoga literally means 'to find union' with God. Since there are a number of ways to do that, yoga practice is divided into a variety of approaches. The Bhagavad-gītā lists the most prominent of them: karma-yoga (the practice of conscious action), jñāna-yoga (the contemplative study of spiritually oriented philosophy), rāja-yoga (yoga asanas and breathing exercises, performed to allow body and mind to rest in meditation on God), and the culmination of these practices, bhakti-yoga. Bhakti-yoga is the most effective and powerful form of yoga because it allows for the fullest expression of the heart.

Bhakti means 'love and devotion' offered to God. When we feel someone loves us, we're willing to let them know us and we reciprocate their love. Similarly, Kṛṣṇa, the Supreme Being, opens His heart to those who love Him. Love for God is inherent in the soul, and bhakti-yogis use body, mind and words to rekindle that love. The foremost bhakti practice is mantra meditation, particularly the chanting of Kṛṣṇa's names. Chanting God's names purifies the heart, calms the mind, gives rise to patience, compassion and kindness, and reawakens our love of God.

What is yoga?

Nowadays people take the goal of yoga to be health. But yoga is not actually meant for that purpose. Yoga is meant to detach us from matter and connect us with the Supreme.

The word *yoga* means 'to join'. Although we are naturally part and parcel of the Supreme, in our conditioned state we are now separated. Because of our separation, we are reluctant to understand God and to speak of our relationship with Him, and we are even inclined to think of such discussion as a waste of time.

The real purpose of practising yoga is to realize that I am not this body. I want eternal happiness, complete knowledge and eternal life – that is the ultimate end of the true yoga system. The goal of yoga is transcendental, beyond both body and mind.

Are there different types of yoga?

In the *Bhagavad-gītā* there are three basic types of yoga delineated – karma-yoga, jñāna-yoga and bhakti-yoga. The systems of yoga may be likened to a staircase. Someone may be on the first step, someone may be halfway up or someone may be on the top step. When one is elevated to certain levels, he is known as a karma-yogi, jñāna-yogi, etc. In all cases, the service to the Supreme Lord is the same. It is a difference in elevation only.

Can you recommend the most practical and evolved form of yoga – what's at the top of the staircase?

When we speak of yoga we refer to linking our consciousness with the Supreme Absolute Truth. Such a process is named differently by various practitioners in terms of the particular method adopted. When the linking process is predominantly in fruitive activities it is called karma-yoga, when it is predominantly empirical it is called jñāna-yoga, and when it is predominantly in a devotional relationship with the Supreme Lord it is called bhakti-yoga. Bhakti-yoga, or Kṛṣṇa consciousness, is the ultimate perfection of all yogas, as will be explained in the *Bhagavad-gītā* (6.47): 'And of all yogis, the one with great faith who always abides in Me, thinks of Me within himself and renders transcendental loving service to Me – he is the most intimately united with Me in yoga and is the highest of all.'

How do you practise bhakti-yoga?

Bhakti means 'devotional service'. Every service has some attractive feature that drives the servitor progressively on and on. Every one of us within this world is perpetually engaged in some sort of service, and the impetus for such service is the pleasure we derive from it.

Devotional service in practice means utilizing our different sensory organs in service to Kṛṣṇa. Some of the senses are meant for acquiring knowledge and some are meant for executing the conclusions of our thinking, feeling and willing. So practice means employing both the mind and the senses in practical devotional service. This practice is not for developing something artificial. For example, a child learns or practises to walk. This walking is not unnatural. The walking capacity is there originally in the child, and simply by a little practice he walks very nicely. Similarly, devotional service to the Supreme Lord is the natural instinct of every living entity.

Does the practice of bhakti-yoga include meditation?

It is generally thought, at least in the Western world, that the yoga system involves meditating on the void. But the Vedic literature does not recommend meditating on any void. Rather, the *Vedas* maintain that yoga means meditation on Viṣṇu (Kṛṣṇa), and this is also maintained in the *Bhagavad-gītā.*

In many yoga societies we find that people sit cross-legged and very straight, then close their eyes to meditate, and so 50 percent of them go to sleep, because when we close our eyes and have no subject matter for contemplation, we simply go to sleep. Of course, this is not recommended by Śrī Kṛṣṇa in the *Bhagavad-gītā.* One must sit very straight, and the eyes should only be half closed, gazing at the tip of one's nose. If one does not follow the instructions, the result will be sleep and nothing more. Sometimes, of course, meditation goes on when one is sleeping, but this is not the recommended process for the execution of yoga. Thus to keep oneself awake Kṛṣṇa advises that one always keep the tip of the nose visible.

In addition, one must be always undisturbed. If the mind is agitated or if there is a great deal of activity going on, one will not be able to concentrate. In meditational yoga one must also be devoid of fear. There is no question of fear when one enters spiritual life. And one must also be *brahmacārī,* completely free from sex life. Nor can there be any demands on one meditating in this way. When there are no demands, and one executes this system properly, then he can control his mind. After one has met all the requirements for meditation, he must transfer his whole thought to Kṛṣṇa, or Viṣṇu. It is not that one is to transfer his thought to vacancy. Thus Kṛṣṇa says that one absorbed in the meditational yoga system is 'always thinking of Me'.

If meditation requires so many things – deep concentration, no fear, no sex – is meditating a practical process?

The *Śrīmad-Bhāgavatam* describes the people of this age. Their duration of life is said to be very short, they tend to be phlegmatic and slow and to sleep a great deal, and when they're not sleeping, they are busy earning money. At the most they only have two hours a day for spiritual activities, so what is the hope for spiritual understanding? It is also stated that even if one is anxious to make spiritual progress, there are many pseudospiritual societies to take advantage of them. People are also characterized in this age as being unfortunate. They have a great deal of difficulty meeting the primary demands of life – eating, defending, mating and sleeping – necessities that are met even by animals. Even if people are meeting these necessities in this age, they are always anxious about war – either defending themselves from aggressors or having to go to war themselves. In addition, there are always disturbing diseases and economic problems. Therefore Lord Śrī Kṛṣṇa considered that in this age it is impossible for people to come to the perfectional stage of liberation by following the rules and regulations prescribed for serious spiritual practice.

Thus out of His causeless mercy, Śrī Kṛṣṇa came as Caitanya Mahāprabhu and distributed the means to the highest perfection of life and spiritual ecstasy through the chanting of Hare Kṛṣṇa, Hare Kṛṣṇa, Kṛṣṇa Kṛṣṇa, Hare Hare / Hare Rāma, Hare Rāma, Rāma Rāma, Hare Hare. This process of chanting is most practical, and it does not depend on whether or not one is liberated or whether or not one's condition is conducive to spiritual life. Whoever takes to this process immediately becomes purified. Therefore the process is called 'pure'. Furthermore, for one who takes to this Kṛṣṇa consciousness process, the seeds of latent reactions to sinful actions are all nullified. Just as fire turns whatever we put into it to ashes, this process turns to ashes all the sinful reactions of our past lives.

So are you saying that chanting is the most essential practice in bhakti-yoga?

All forms of yoga are meant for transcendental life, but the method of chanting is especially effective in this age. *Kīrtana* may go on for hours, and one may not feel tired, but it is difficult to sit in the lotus position perfectly still for more than a few minutes.

A yogi obviously has to go through a great deal of difficulty to purify the mind, body and soul, but it is a fact that this can be done most effectively in this age simply by the chanting of Hare Kṛṣṇa, Hare Kṛṣṇa, Kṛṣṇa Kṛṣṇa, Hare Hare / Hare Rāma, Hare Rāma, Rāma Rāma, Hare Hare. Why? Because this transcendental sound vibration is nondifferent from Kṛṣṇa. When we chant Kṛṣṇa's name with devotion, then He is with us, and when Kṛṣṇa is with us, then what is the possibility of remaining impure? Consequently, one absorbed in Kṛṣṇa consciousness, in chanting the names of Kṛṣṇa and serving Him always, receives the benefit of the highest form of yoga. The advantage is that he doesn't have to take all the trouble of the meditational process. That is the beauty of Kṛṣṇa consciousness.

But can I do this essential practice?
What if I'm just beginning yoga?

If somebody who wants to reach the hundredth floor is given a chance to use the elevator, within a minute he will be able to come to the top. Of course, he may still say, 'Why should I take advantage of this elevator? I shall go step by step.' He can do this, but there is a chance he will not reach the top floor. Similarly, if one takes help from the 'elevator' of bhakti-yoga, within a short time he can reach the hundredth floor, the perfection of yoga, Kṛṣṇa consciousness.

Kṛṣṇa consciousness is the direct process. You may go step by step, following all the other yoga systems, or you may take directly to Kṛṣṇa consciousness. Lord Caitanya has recommended that in this age, since people are very short-lived, disturbed and full of anxiety, they should take up the direct process. And by His grace, by His causeless mercy, He has given us the chanting of the Hare Kṛṣṇa mantra, which lifts us immediately to the platform of bhakti-yoga. It is immediate; we don't have to wait. That is the special gift of Lord Caitanya.

The only way to know God in truth is through bhakti-yoga. In the *Bhagavad-gītā* (18.55) Kṛṣṇa confirms this: 'Only by devotional service can one understand the Supreme Personality of Godhead as He is.' The *Vedas* confirm that only through bhakti, or devotional service, can one attain the highest perfectional stage. If one practises other yoga systems, they must be mixed with bhakti if one is to make any progress. But because people don't have sufficient time to execute all the practices of any other yoga system, the direct process of bhakti-yoga, unadulterated devotion, is recommended for this age. Therefore it is by great fortune that one comes to Kṛṣṇa consciousness, the path of bhakti-yoga, and becomes well situated according to the Vedic directions.

What is the result of chanting Hare Kṛṣṇa?

The more one goes on chanting, the more the darkness accrued over many lives is dissipated. By chanting, one can cleanse the dust from the mirror of his mind and perceive things very distinctly. Thus one will know what he is, what God is, what this world is, what our relationship with God in this world is, how to live in this world and what our next life is.

Why is the mantra so powerful?

This transcendental sound vibration will immediately carry you to the transcendental platform, especially if you try to hear so that your mind is absorbed in the sound. This Hare Kṛṣṇa sound vibration is nondifferent from Kṛṣṇa because Kṛṣṇa is absolute. Since God is absolute, there is no difference between God's name and God Himself. In the material world there is a difference between water and the word *water,* between a flower and the word *flower.* But in the spiritual world, in the absolute world, there is no such difference. Therefore as soon as you vibrate Hare Kṛṣṇa, Hare Kṛṣṇa, you immediately associate with the Supreme Lord and His energy.

The sound Kṛṣṇa and the original Kṛṣṇa are the same. When we chant Hare Kṛṣṇa and dance, Kṛṣṇa is also dancing with us. Of course, we may say, 'Well, I do not see Him,' but why do we put so much stress on seeing? Why not hearing? Seeing, tasting, smelling, touching and hearing are all instruments for experience and knowledge. Why do we put such exclusive stress on seeing? A devotee does not wish to see Kṛṣṇa; he is satisfied by simply hearing of Kṛṣṇa. Seeing may eventually be there, but hearing should not be considered any less important. There are things we hear but do not see – the wind may be whistling past our ears and we can hear it, but there is no possibility of seeing the wind. Since hearing is no less an important experience than seeing, and it is no less valid, we can hear Kṛṣṇa and realize His presence through sound. Śrī Kṛṣṇa Himself says, 'I am not there in My abode or in the heart of the meditating yogi; I am where my pure devotees are singing My names.' We can feel the presence of Kṛṣṇa as we make progress.

Can anyone chant Hare Kṛṣṇa?

That is the beauty of this Kṛṣṇa consciousness movement. It is not simply for one age or for one country or for one class of people. Hare Kṛṣṇa can be chanted by any man in any social position, in any country and in any age, for Kṛṣṇa is the Supreme Lord of all people in all social positions, in all countries, in all ages.

It seems chanting mantras could become repetitive.

Our students can chant the Hare Kṛṣṇa mantra twenty-four hours a day and they will never get tired. They will continue to dance and chant. Anyone can try it; because it is not material, one will never get tired of chanting Hare Kṛṣṇa. In the material world, if one chants anything, any favourite name, for three, four or ten times, he will get tired of it. That is a fact. But because Hare Kṛṣṇa is not material, if one chants this mantra he will never get tired. The more one chants, the more his heart will be cleansed of material dirt and the more the problems of his life within this material world will be solved.

What if I don't feel attracted to chanting?

If a man is suffering from jaundice and you give him a piece of sugar candy, he will say that it is very bitter. But is sugar candy bitter? No, it is very sweet. And the medicine for jaundice is that sugar. Modern science prescribes this, and it is prescribed in the Vedic literature also. So if we take a great quantity of this sugar candy, then we will be relieved from jaundice. And when there is relief, then one says, 'Oh, this is very sweet.' So the modern jaundice of a godless civilization can be cured by this chanting of Hare Kṛṣṇa. In the beginning it may appear bitter, but when one advances, then he will see how pleasing it is.

Is chanting a form of self-hypnosis?

Kṛṣṇa consciousness is not an artificial imposition on the mind. This consciousness is the original natural energy of the living entity. When we hear the transcendental vibration, this consciousness is revived. This simplest method of meditation is recommended for this age. By practical experience also, one can perceive that by chanting this *mahā-mantra,* or the 'great chanting for deliverance', one can at once feel a transcendental ecstasy coming through from the spiritual stratum. In the material concept of life we are busy in the matter of sense gratification as if we were in the lower animal stage. A little elevated from this status of sense gratification, one is engaged in mental speculation for the purpose of getting out of the material clutches. A little elevated from this speculative status, when one is intelligent enough, one tries to find out the supreme cause of all causes – within and without. And when one is factually on the plane of spiritual understanding, surpassing the stages of sense, mind and intelligence, he is then on the transcendental plane. This chanting of the Hare Kṛṣṇa mantra is enacted from the spiritual platform, and thus this sound vibration surpasses all lower strata of consciousness – namely sensual, mental and intellectual. There is no need, therefore, to understand the language of the mantra, nor is there any need for mental speculation nor any intellectual adjustment for chanting this *mahā-mantra.* It is automatic, from the spiritual platform, and as such, anyone can take part in vibrating this transcendental sound without any previous qualification.

What do the words in the Hare Kṛṣṇa mantra mean?

Rāma and Kṛṣṇa are names of God, and Hare is the energy of God. So when we chant the *mahā-mantra,* we address God together with His energy. This energy is of two kinds, the spiritual and the material. At present we are in the clutches of the material energy. Therefore we pray to Kṛṣṇa that He may kindly deliver us from the service of the material energy and accept us into the service of the spiritual energy. That is our whole philosophy. Hare Kṛṣṇa means, 'O energy of God, O God [Kṛṣṇa], please engage me in Your service.' It is our nature to render service. Somehow or other we have come to the service of material things, but when this service is transformed into the service of the spiritual energy, then our life is perfect. To practise bhakti-yoga, loving service to God, means to become free from designations like 'Hindu', 'Muslim', 'Christian', this or that, and simply to serve God. We have created the Christian, Hindu and Islamic religions, but when we come to a religion without designations – in which we don't think we are Hindus or Christians or Muslims – then we can speak of pure religion, or bhakti.

Do I have to change my life to practise this kind of mantra meditation?

You do not have to change your situation. If you are a student, remain a student. If you are a businessman, remain a businessman. Woman, man, black, white – anyone can chant Hare Kṛṣṇa. It is a simple process and there is no charge. We are not saying, 'Give me so many dollars, and I shall give you this Hare Kṛṣṇa mantra.' No, we are distributing it publicly. You simply have to catch it up and try it. You'll very quickly come to the transcendental platform. When you hear the chanting, that is transcendental meditation.

This process is recommended in all the scriptures of the Vedic literature. It was taught by Lord Caitanya and followed by His disciplic succession for the last five hundred years, and people are achieving good results from it today, not only in India but here also. So our request is that you give it a try. Why should you try for any hard process? Simply chant Hare Kṛṣṇa, Hare Kṛṣṇa, Kṛṣṇa Kṛṣṇa, Hare Hare / Hare Rāma, Hare Rāma, Rāma Rāma, Hare Hare. And you can chant twenty-four hours a day.

Are there rules I should follow while chanting Hare Kṛṣṇa?

Kṛṣṇa proclaims that yoga cannot be properly performed by one who eats too much or eats too little. One who starves himself cannot properly perform yoga. Nor can the person who eats more than required. The eating process should be moderate – just enough to keep body and soul together; it should not be for the enjoyment of the tongue. Nor can one execute the meditational yoga system if one sleeps too much or does not sleep sufficiently. Thus Kṛṣṇa outlines so many requirements for disciplining the body. All these requirements, however, can essentially be broken down into four basic rules: no illicit sexual connection, no intoxication, no meat-eating and no gambling. These are the four minimum regulations for the execution of any yoga system. And who in this age can refrain from these activities? We have to test ourselves accordingly to ascertain our success in yoga execution.

Will meditation help me become more peaceful?

It is because the mind is agitated and not fixed on Kṛṣṇa that it goes from one thought to another. For instance, when we are engaged in work, memories of events that happened ten, twenty, thirty or forty years ago may suddenly come to our mind for no apparent reason. These thoughts come from our subconscious, and because they are always rising, the mind is always agitated. If we agitate a lake or a pond, all the mud from the bottom comes to the surface. Similarly, when the mind is agitated, so many thoughts arise from the subconscious that have been stored there over the years. If we do not disturb a pond, the mud will settle to the bottom. This yoga process is the means to quiet the mind and allow all these thoughts to settle. For this reason there are so many rules and regulations to follow in order to keep the mind from becoming agitated. If we follow the rules and regulations, gradually the mind will come under control. There are so many don'ts and so many dos, and if one is serious about training the mind, he has to follow them. If he acts whimsically, what is the possibility of the mind being controlled? When the mind is finally trained to the point where it will think of nothing but Kṛṣṇa, it will attain peace and will become very tranquil.

What is the primary quality I have to develop if I want to practise spiritual life?

We should be very serious about attaining our eternal life full of bliss and knowledge. We have forgotten that this is actually our aim of life, our real self-interest. Why have we forgotten? We have simply been entrapped by the material glitter, by skyscrapers, big factories and political play, although we know that however big we build skyscrapers, we will not be able to live here indefinitely. We should not spoil our energy in building mighty industries and cities to further entrap ourselves in material nature; rather, our energy should be used to develop Kṛṣṇa consciousness in order to attain a spiritual body whereby we may enter into Kṛṣṇa's planet. Kṛṣṇa consciousness is not a religious formula or some spiritual recreation; it is the most important part of the living entity.

Do I need a guru?

When a physician is seriously sick, he does not prescribe his own treatment. He knows his brain is not in order, so he calls for another physician. Similarly, when we are perplexed, bewildered, when we cannot reach any solution – at that time the right person to search out is the guru. It is essential; you cannot avoid it. So, in our present state of existence we are all perplexed. And under the circumstances, a guru is required to give us real direction.

Unfortunately, our disease is that we are rebellious – we automatically resist authority. Yet although we say that we don't want authority, nature is so strong that it forces authority upon us. We are forced to accept the authority of nature. What can be more pathetic than a man who claims to answer to no authority but who follows his senses blindly wherever they lead him? Our false claim to independence is simply foolishness. We are all under authority, yet we say that we don't want authority. This is called *māyā*, illusion. We do, however, have a certain independence – we can choose to be under the authority of our senses or the authority of

Kṛṣṇa. The best and ultimate authority is Kṛṣṇa, for He is our eternal well-wisher and He always speaks for our benefit. Since we have to accept some authority, why not accept His?

Can't I be my own guru?

Of course, no one likes to surrender to anyone. We are puffed up with whatever knowledge we have, and our attitude is, 'Oh, who can give me knowledge?' Some people say that for spiritual realization there is no need for a spiritual master, but so far as Vedic literature is concerned, and as far as the *Bhagavad-gītā, Śrīmad-Bhāgavatam* and the *Upaniṣads* are concerned, there is need of a spiritual master. Even in the material world if one wants to learn to be a musician, he has to search out a musician to teach him, or if one wants to be an engineer, he has to go to a technological college and learn from those who know the technology. Nor can anyone become a doctor by simply purchasing a book from the market and reading it at home. One has to be admitted to a medical college and undergo training under licensed doctors. It is not possible to learn any major subject simply by purchasing books and reading them at home. Someone is needed to show us how to apply the knowledge found in the books. As far as the science of God is concerned, Śrī Kṛṣṇa, the Supreme Personality of Godhead Himself, advises us to go to a person to whom we can surrender. This means that we have to check to see if a person is capable of giving instructions on the *Bhagavad-gītā* and other texts discussing God realization. It is not that we are to search out a spiritual master whimsically. We should be very serious to find a person who is actually in knowledge of the subject.

What can I get from a guru?

A living being who lives in the mundane world has four defects: (1) he is certain to commit mistakes; (2) he is subject to illusion;

(3) he has a propensity to cheat others; and (4) his senses are imperfect. No one with these four imperfections can deliver perfect knowledge. The *Vedas* are not produced by such an imperfect creature. Vedic knowledge was originally imparted by the Lord into the heart of Brahmā, the first created living being, and Brahmā in his turn disseminated this knowledge to his sons and disciples, who have handed it down through history.

A bona fide guru does not impart some self-styled, concocted knowledge; his knowledge is standard and received from the system of disciplic succession of spiritual masters. He is also firmly fixed in the service of the Supreme Personality of Godhead. These are his two qualifications: he must have heard the Vedic knowledge through the disciplic succession, and he must be established in service to the Supreme Lord. He does not have to be a very learned scholar, but he must have heard from the proper authority.

How can I avoid being cheated by a fake guru?

If we want to purchase something, we must at least have some idea of what that thing is. Otherwise we will be cheated. If we want to purchase a mango from the market, we must at least know what type of food a mango is and what it looks like. Similarly, we must have some preliminary knowledge of the qualifications of a bona fide spiritual master. The *Bhagavad-gītā* gives some information about the succession of spiritual masters.

What are the qualities of an advanced spiritualist?

Anyone who has developed unalloyed, unflinching devotional service to the Lord develops his original good qualities as spirit soul. The spirit soul, as part and parcel of the Supreme Personality of Godhead, has all the good qualities of the Lord. These qualities of a devotee, twenty-six in number, are listed as follows: (1) he is kind to everyone, (2) does not quarrel with anyone, (3) is

The body changes from one form to another, but the soul exists eternally without change. Our material body began in the womb of our mother and has been changing shape ever since – a process we call 'growth' but which is really a changing body. Although we have changed our body many times – we can each remember being babies and then children – we are the same person because we are not our body but the soul. (p. 10)

We've created a humbug civilization. We try to make ourselves comfortable but only make ourselves uncomfortable. Every year we manufacture cars, which means we have to build roads, which we then have to repair at great cost and inconvenience. Problem after problem, and all in pursuit of an illusory happiness. We try to be happy, but we succeed only in creating new problems. This is the nature of the material world. (pp. 13–14)

The *Bhagavad-gītā* speaks of a tree whose roots grow upward and its branches downward. We can all see such a tree. Trees reflected in water are upside down. The tree's reflection has no substance – it's a shadow tree. Like the upside-down tree, the material world is a reflection of the spiritual world. And like the tree's reflection, the material world has no substance but shows us a reflection of the spiritual world. (p. 21)

The goal of yoga is to transcend body and mind. Practising yoga is meant to help us realize that we're not the body; we're spiritual beings. As spiritual beings, it's natural to want eternal happiness, complete knowledge and eternal life, and attaining these is the ultimate goal of the yoga system. (p. 56)

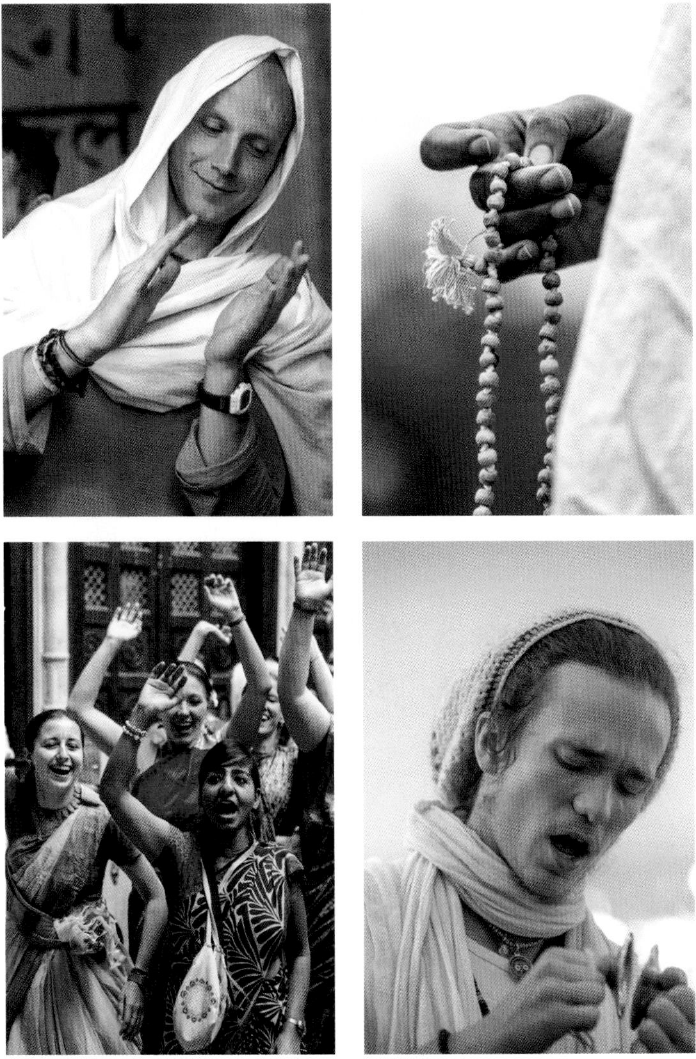

Kṛṣṇa consciousness is not an artificial imposition on the mind but our original, natural energy. When we hear transcendental vibration, our natural, spiritual consciousness is revived. The simplest method of meditation recommended for this age is to chant the Hare Kṛṣṇa *mahā-mantra*, the 'great chant for deliverance'. Those who chant can at once feel a transcendental ecstasy coming through from the spiritual stratum. (pp. 63–64)

Learn to see all beings with compassion, as equals. Work to benefit others. Those who understand that all beings are part of God, even though their karma may have given them bodies different from ours, don't discriminate: 'This is an animal, so it should be sent to the slaughterhouse so we can eat it.' Why should animals be killed? Bhakti-yogis are kind to everyone. A tenet of the Kṛṣṇa conscious philosophy is no meat-eating. (p. 77)

Do I need a guru? When doctors are sick, they don't treat themselves but call for other doctors. Similarly, when we're bewildered and can't solve our deeper problems we should seek out a guru. Guidance from a bona fide guru is essential; we can't avoid it if we wish to solve life's perplexities. In our present state we are all perplexed by our own unhappiness. Under the circumstances, we need a guru to give us real direction. (p. 68)

Sacred places and images inspire bhakti. Here, Rādhā-Gokulānanda grace the sacred altar at Bhaktivedanta Manor, a Tudor mansion in Hertfordshire donated to the Hare Kṛṣṇa movement in 1973 by Beatle George Harrison. Over the years the Manor has become a thriving spiritual centre. The Manor attracts bhakti-yogis from across the UK for joyful chanting and meditation sessions.

fixed in the Absolute Truth, (4) equal to everyone, (5) faultless, (6) charitable, (7) mild, (8) clean, (9) simple, (10) benevolent, (11) peaceful, (12) completely attached to Kṛṣṇa, (13) has no material hankering, (14) is meek, (15) steady, (16) self-controlled, (17) does not eat more than required, (18) is sane, (19) respectful, (20) humble, (21) grave, (22) compassionate, (23) friendly, (24) poetic, (25) expert, (26) silent.

What if the guru says he's God?

The spiritual master will never say, 'I am God – I can give you mercy.' No. That is not a spiritual master; that is a bogus pretender. The spiritual master will say, 'I am a servant of God; I have brought His mercy. Please take it and be satisfied.' This is the spiritual master's business. He is just like a postman. When a postman delivers you some large amount of money, it is not his own money. The money is sent by someone else, but he honestly delivers it – 'Sir, here is your money. Take it.' So you become very much satisfied with him, although it is not his money he is giving you. When you are in need and you get money from your father or someone else – brought by the postman – you feel very much satisfied.

Similarly, we are all suffering in this blazing fire of material existence. But the spiritual master brings the message from the Supreme Lord and delivers it to you, and if you kindly accept it, then you'll be satisfied. This is the business of the spiritual master.

Why is a guru given so much respect?

When we offer respects to the guru, we are offering respects to God. Because we are trying to be God conscious, it is required that we learn how to offer respects to God through God's representative. In all the scriptures, the guru is said to be as good as God, but the guru never says, 'I am God.' The disciple's duty is to offer respect to the guru just as he offers respect to God, but the guru never thinks, 'My disciples are offering me the same respect they offer to God; therefore I have become God.' As soon as he thinks like this he becomes a dog instead of God.

Do spiritual people suffer?

No one can adjust the sufferings of material existence, but by spiritual culture one can elevate himself from the effects of such miserable life. As an example one may cite the condition of a dry coconut. The dry coconut pulp automatically becomes separated from its outer skin. Similarly, the outer skin, or the gross and subtle material coverings of the soul, automatically separates from the spirit soul, and the spirit soul can then exist in spiritual existence, even though apparently within the dry skin. This freedom from the false sense of ego is called the liberation of the soul.

I have a busy life. Can't I wait until I'm old to take up serious spiritual practice?

It is important to take to Kṛṣṇa consciousness immediately, because we do not know how much time is left before death. When your time in this body expires, no one can stop your death. The arrangement of material nature is so strong. You cannot say, 'Let me remain.' Actually, people sometimes request like that. When I was in Allahabad, an old friend who was very rich was dying. At that time he begged the doctor, 'Can't you give me at least four more years to live? I have some plans I could not finish.' This is foolishness. Everyone thinks, 'Oh, I have to do this. I have to do that.' No. Neither the doctors nor the scientists can check death: 'Oh, no, sir. Not four years. Not even four minutes. You have to go immediately.' This is the law. So before that moment comes, one should be very careful to become realized in Kṛṣṇa consciousness. You should realize Kṛṣṇa consciousness very quickly. Before your next death comes, you must finish your business. That is intelligence. Otherwise you will suffer defeat.

What if I don't perfect my spiritual consciousness in this life?

In the material world, we have experience that we do not carry our assets from one life to another. I may have millions of dollars in the bank, but as soon as my body is finished, my bank balance is also. At death, the bank balance does not go with me; it remains in the bank to be enjoyed by somebody else. This is not the case with spiritual culture. Even if one enacts a very small amount on the spiritual platform, he takes that with him to his next life and picks up again from that point.

When one picks up this knowledge that was interrupted, he should know that he should now finish the balance and complete the yogic process. One should not take the chance of finishing up the process in another birth but should resolve to finish it in this life. We should be determined in this way: 'Somehow or other in my last life, I did not finish my spiritual cultivation. Now Kṛṣṇa has given me another opportunity, so let me finish it up in this life.' Thus after leaving this body one will not again take birth in this material world, where birth, old age, disease and death are omnipresent, but will return to Kṛṣṇa. Once one has approached Kṛṣṇa and has attempted to make spiritual progress, Kṛṣṇa, who is situated in the heart, begins to give directions. In the *Bhagavad-gītā* Śrī Kṛṣṇa says that for one who wants to remember Him, He gives remembrance, and for one who wants to forget Him, He allows him to forget.

Why do some people give up their spiritual practices?

This combination of Kṛṣṇa and the spiritual master is the cause of one's receiving the seed of Kṛṣṇa consciousness. Where should you sow that seed? If you have information of Kṛṣṇa consciousness, you just sow it in your heart. Not in this earth, but in the earth within yourself. And after sowing a seed you have to pour a little water on it. That water is hearing and chanting [about Kṛṣṇa]. Once the seed is sown in the heart, just pour on a little water and it will grow.

If you stop pouring water on a plant, it will dry up and will not produce any fruit. Similarly, even if you are highly elevated in Kṛṣṇa consciousness, you cannot stop this process of hearing and chanting because *māyā* is so strong, so powerful, that as soon as she sees, 'Ah, here is an opportunity', at once you will dry up. By the process of pouring water, that plant of Kṛṣṇa consciousness grows.

I've been trying to keep up my spiritual practice, but I feel stagnant.

It is not possible to make progress as long as our desires are anchored in the material world. In this regard, there is a story of a bridegroom's party who had to go to the bride's house down the river. It was settled that they would start at night by boat and reach the destination early in the morning. Therefore at night, after supper, the jubilant party got aboard a boat, made themselves comfortable, and instructed the boatmen to start. Since all the members of the party were seated comfortably, and since the river breeze was very pleasant, they slept soundly that night. In the morning they all got up early, but to their astonishment they saw that the boat had not moved an inch toward the destination, even though the boatmen had rowed vigorously all night long. Finally, after inquiring, they found that despite the boatmen's rowing, the boat had not moved because they had failed to raise the anchor. The marriage ceremony was thus spoiled because of a foolish mistake.

The different weights on the anchor that keep us grounded in material life are our attachment to the material body due to our ignorance of spiritual facts, our attachment to kinsmen due to bodily relations, our attachment to our land of birth and our material possessions, our attachments to material science and our attachments to religious forms and rituals, which we follow without knowing their true purpose. All these anchor the boat of the human body to the material universe.

How can I make my spiritual development feel both serious and exciting?

A devotee should execute his devotional services with full energy, endurance and confidence. He should perform his scheduled duties, he should be pure in heart, and he should serve in association with devotees. All six of these items will lead the devotee to the path of success. One should not be discouraged in the discharge of devotional service. Failures may not be detrimental; they may be the pillars of success. One must have good faith in the regulative principles followed by the self-realized souls, and one should not be doubtful about the ultimate result of such devotional service. Rather, one must go on executing his prescribed duties without hesitation, and one should never be influenced by unwanted association. We should not consider going back to Godhead a plaything. We must take it seriously, as enjoined in the scriptures. For a strict follower, the result is sure and certain, and when the time is right the result will come of its own force.

When will I see Kṛṣṇa?

We should always think of Kṛṣṇa, and when we attain perfection we shall see Kṛṣṇa before us. This is the process. We should not be too hasty. We should wait for the mature time. Of course, it is good to be eager to see Kṛṣṇa, but we should not become discouraged if we do not see Him immediately. If a woman gets married and wants a child immediately, she will be disappointed. It is not possible to have a child immediately. She must wait. Similarly, we cannot expect that just because we engage ourselves in Kṛṣṇa consciousness we can see Kṛṣṇa immediately. But we must have faith that we will see Him. We must have firm faith that because we are engaged in Kṛṣṇa consciousness we shall be able to see Kṛṣṇa face to face. We should not be disappointed. We should simply go on with our Kṛṣṇa conscious activities, and the time will come when we will see Kṛṣṇa. There is no doubt about this.

Will practising Kṛṣṇa consciousness make me a better person?

It is a fact that whoever takes to Kṛṣṇa consciousness does not have to endeavour independently to become a good man. All the good qualifications will automatically come. It is stated in *Śrīmad-Bhāgavatam* that one who has attained Kṛṣṇa consciousness has simultaneously attained all good qualities. On the other hand, if a person is devoid of God consciousness and yet has many good qualities, his good qualities are to be considered useless, for he will not in any way be prohibited from doing that which is undesirable. If one is devoid of Kṛṣṇa consciousness, he is sure to commit mischief in this material world.

Do I have to follow your culture and lifestyle to be spiritual?

The saffron robes and the shaven head [of the monks in the Kṛṣṇa consciousness movement] are not essential, but adopting them creates a good mental situation, just as when a military man is dressed properly he gets energy – he feels like a military man. Does that mean that unless he is in uniform he cannot fight? No. In the same way, God consciousness cannot be checked – it can be revived in any circumstances – but certain conditions are helpful. Therefore we prescribe that you live in a certain way, dress in a certain way, eat in a certain way and so on. These things are helpful for practising Kṛṣṇa consciousness, but they are not essential.

How do you eat in Kṛṣṇa consciousness?

The whole process of bhakti-yoga is meant to purify us, and eating is part of that purification. I think you have a saying, 'You are what you eat', and that's a fact. Our bodily constitution and mental atmosphere are determined according to how and what we eat. Therefore the scriptures recommend that to become Kṛṣṇa conscious you should eat remnants of food left by Kṛṣṇa. If a tuberculosis patient eats something and you eat the remnants, you will be infected with tuberculosis. Similarly, if you eat *kṛṣṇa-prasāda,* then you will be infected with Kṛṣṇa consciousness. Thus our process is that we don't eat anything immediately. First we offer the food to Kṛṣṇa, and then we eat it. This helps us advance in Kṛṣṇa consciousness.

Kṛṣṇa can eat anything because He is God, but in the *Bhagavad-gītā* (9.26) He says, 'If one offers Me with love and devotion a leaf, a flower, fruit or water, I will accept it.' He never says, 'Give Me meat and wine.'

Why don't you eat meat?

One who is learned sees all living entities on an equal level. Therefore, because a devotee of Kṛṣṇa is learned, he is also compassionate and can work in such a way as to actually benefit humanity. A devotee feels and actually sees that all living entities are part and parcel of God and that somehow or other they have fallen into contact with this material world and have assumed different types of bodies according to their different karmas.

Those who are learned do not discriminate between them. They do not say, 'This is an animal, so it should be sent to the slaughter-house so that a man may eat it.' No. Why should the animals be slaughtered? A person who is actually Kṛṣṇa conscious is kind to everyone. Therefore one tenet of our philosophy is no meat-eating.

In the *Bhagavad-gītā* the Lord has expressed His willingness to accept fruit, flowers, leaves and water from His devotees when they have been offered to Him in devotional affection. The Lord can eat anything and everything, because everything is but a transformation of His own energy. But when there is a question of offering Him something, the offerings must be within the range of the eatables the Lord has ordered. We cannot offer the Lord that which He has not ordered. The Personality of Godhead, Śrī Kṛṣṇa, cannot be offered anything beyond the range of good foods like rice, dal [beans and legumes], wheat, vegetables, milk and milk preparations and sugar.

I know that yoga has dos and don'ts and one of them is related to sex. What are your views on sex?

The whole system of materialistic life revolves around this sexual pleasure. But this pleasure is like one drop of water in the desert. The desert requires an ocean of water. If you find one drop of water in a desert, you can certainly say, 'Here is some water.' But what is its value? Similarly, there is certainly some pleasure in sex life, but what is the value of that pleasure? Compared to the unlimited pleasure of Kṛṣṇa consciousness, it is like one drop of water in the desert. Everyone is seeking unlimited pleasure, but no one is becoming satisfied.

Do I need to renounce everything I'm doing and have in order to be spiritual?

Real renunciation means to give up the process of sense gratification and apply yourself very seriously in the service of the Lord. In other words, renunciation means not to try to give up this world but to work in this world and give the fruits of our work to the service of Kṛṣṇa. Everyone is working in this material world to get some result. Whether you work piously or impiously, there must be some result. Nondevotees try to enjoy the result and become entangled, whereas devotees give the fruits of their labours to Kṛṣṇa and are liberated.

Can we use our material things in the service of God?

Everything used in Kṛṣṇa's service is spiritual. For example, each day we distribute fruit that has been offered to Kṛṣṇa (*prasāda*). Now, one may ask, 'Why is this fruit different from ordinary fruit? It has been purchased at the market like any other fruit. We also eat fruit at home. What is the difference?' No. Because we offer the fruit to Kṛṣṇa, it immediately becomes spiritual. The result? Just go on eating *kṛṣṇa-prasāda* and you will see how you are making progress in Kṛṣṇa consciousness.

Here is another example. If you drink a large quantity of milk there may be some disorder in your bowels. If you go to a physician (at least, if you go to an Ayurvedic physician), he'll offer you a medicinal preparation made with yogurt. And that yogurt with a little medicine in it will cure you. Now, yogurt is nothing but milk transformed. So, your disease was caused by milk and it is also cured by milk. How is that? Because you are taking the medicine under the direction of a qualified physician. Similarly, if you engage the material energy in the service of Kṛṣṇa under the direction of a bona fide spiritual master, that same material energy that has been the cause of your bondage will bring you to the transcendental stage beyond all misery.

8

Yogic Perfection – Living the Dream

The Vedic texts offer enchanting accounts of the metaphysical world. In that realm, every step is a dance, every word is a song, every action is motivated by pure love and the atmosphere is infused with ever-increasing transcendental happiness. Sounds good. Maybe too good? Are these accounts fairy-tale formulations to distract us from the existential aches and pains of the 'real' world? Or could there be a reality beyond the world we see around us?

It's natural for humans to long for a land of purity and safety, peace and love. Instead of simply dismissing these private longings as childish or naïve, it may be worth exploring where such a universal longing comes from. Why is the yearning for immortality and unimpeded happiness so common? As C. S. Lewis famously remarked, 'If I find in myself desires which nothing in this world can satisfy, the only logical explanation is that I was made for another world.'

What is the perfection of life?

If we leave this material body in Kṛṣṇa consciousness, we will no longer have to return to the material world. The point is to avoid this material existence altogether. It is not a question of improving our condition in the material world. In prison a man may want to improve his condition to become a first-class prisoner, and the government may give him A status, but no sane man will become satisfied by becoming an A-class prisoner. He should desire to get out of the prison altogether. In the material world some of us are A-class, B-class, and C-class prisoners, but in any case we are all prisoners.

From the *Bhagavad-gītā* we have to accept that there is a spiritual universe, a kingdom of God. If somehow we are transported to a country where we are informed that we will no longer have to undergo birth, old age, disease and death, will we not be happy? If we heard of such a place, surely we would try as hard as possible to go there. No one wants to grow old; no one wants to die. Indeed, a place free of such sufferings would be our heart's desire. Why do we want this? Because we have the right, the prerogative, to want it. We are eternal, blissful and full of knowledge, but having been covered by this material entanglement, we have forgotten ourselves. Therefore the *Bhagavad-gītā* gives us the advantage of being able to revive our original status.

In yoga, isn't liberation about merging into the 'oneness'?

As living entities we want enjoyment. Being, in itself, is not enough. We want bliss as well as being. In his entirety, the living entity is composed of three qualities – eternality, knowledge and bliss. Those who enter impersonally into the white light surrounding the Lord can remain there for some time in full knowledge that they are now merged homogeneously with Brahman, but they cannot have that eternal bliss, because that part is wanting. One may remain alone in a room for some time and enjoy himself by reading a book or engaging in some thought, but it is not possible to remain in that room for years and years at a time, and certainly not for all eternity. Therefore, for one who merges impersonally into the existence of the Supreme, there is every chance of falling down again into the material world in order to acquire some association.

Should we fear death?

In the *Bhagavad-gītā* (2.13) Kṛṣṇa says that a sober person is not perplexed at the time of death. If you prepare yourself for death, why should you be perplexed? For example, if in your childhood and boyhood you prepare yourself nicely, if you become educated, then you will get a nice job, a nice situation, and be happy. Similarly, if you prepare yourself in this life for going back home, back to Godhead, then where is your perplexity at the time of death? There is no perplexity. You'll know, 'I am going to Kṛṣṇa. I am going back home, back to Godhead. Now I'll not have to change material bodies; I'll have my spiritual body. Now I shall play with Kṛṣṇa and dance with Kṛṣṇa and eat with Kṛṣṇa.' This is Kṛṣṇa consciousness – to prepare yourself for the next life.

How can I enter the spiritual world?

We are eternally connected with the Supreme Lord, but somehow or other we are now in material contamination. Therefore we must take up a process by which to go back again to the spiritual world. That linking process is called yoga. The actual translation of the word *yoga* is 'plus'. At the present moment we are minus God, or minus the Supreme. But when we make ourselves plus – connected – then our human form of life is perfect. During our lifetime we have to practise approaching that point of perfection, and at the time of death, when we give up this material body, that perfection has to be realized. At the time of death one must be prepared. Students, for instance, prepare for two to five years in college, and the final test of their education is the examination. If they pass the examination, they get a degree. Similarly, in the subject of life, if we prepare for the examination at the time of death and pass it, then we are transferred to the spiritual world. Everything is examined at the time of death.

What qualifications do we need if we wish to enter the spiritual world?

The preliminary qualification for going back to Godhead is given in the *Bhagavad-gītā* (15.5): 'One who is free from illusion, false prestige and false association, who understands the eternal, who is done with material lust and is free from the duality of happiness and distress, and who knows how to surrender to the Supreme Person, attains that eternal kingdom.' One who is convinced of his spiritual identity and is freed from the material conception of existence, who is free from illusion and is transcendental to the modes of material nature, who constantly engages in understanding spiritual knowledge and who has completely severed himself from sense enjoyment, can go back to Godhead.

Is the spiritual world anything like the material world?

Here in this material world we create an imitation: the same type of lovers, friends, parents, children – but it is all false. In the desert an animal may see a vast mass of water, but it is only a mirage, and when the animal goes to drink the water, it dies. Similarly, in this material world we are trying to become happy by society, friendship and love, but this is a will-o'-the-wisp, a false thing. Real life is in the society of Kṛṣṇa. Śrīla Bhaktivinoda Ṭhākura, a teacher of Kṛṣṇa consciousness, therefore says, 'If you enter into the society, friendship and love of Kṛṣṇa, that is the perfection of life.' You will not find real happiness in earth, water, fire, air and so on. They are Kṛṣṇa's separated energies. They are a reflection, a false representation, a shadow. For example, when you see your face in the mirror, it is not actually your face you are seeing. It is simply the reflection of your face. Similarly, this material world is just like a reflection of the real, spiritual world. Therefore the material world is known as Kṛṣṇa's separated energy.

So do I have to give up the material world to reach the spiritual world?

The philosophy of Kṛṣṇa consciousness is that although the elements of this material world are separated from Kṛṣṇa, we can use them in service to Kṛṣṇa and thus spiritualize them. A tape recorder is material, but it can be used for Kṛṣṇa's purpose. That is how we are writing books – recording them on a tape recorder. This is proper renunciation. There is no need to give up this earth, water, fire and air, as the impersonalist philosophers say. You can utilize them in Kṛṣṇa's service. After all, they are all Kṛṣṇa's energy.

Then, although this earth, water, fire and air are Kṛṣṇa's separated energies, when we reconnect them by engaging them in the service of the Lord, they become spiritual. Another example: if you put an iron rod into a fire, the rod becomes warm, warmer, warmer, warmer. Then, when it is red-hot, it is no longer an iron rod; it is fire. Similarly, although everything in this material world is separated from Kṛṣṇa, if you engage the things of this world in the service of Kṛṣṇa, they are no longer material; they are spiritual.

Why is the spiritual world so special?

On the absolute plane there is no exploitation. Everyone wants to serve; no one wants to take service. In the transcendental world, everyone wants to give service. You want to give service to me, and I want to give service to you. This is such a nice attitude. This material world means that I want to pickpocket you, and you want to pickpocket me. That's all. This is the material world. We should try to understand it. In the material world, everyone wants to exploit his friend, his father, his mother, everyone. But in the transcendental world, everyone wants to serve. Everyone has Kṛṣṇa as the central point of serving, and all the devotees, either as friends or servants or parents or lovers of Kṛṣṇa, all want to serve Him. And at the same time, Kṛṣṇa also wants to serve them. This is a transcendental relationship; the main function is service, although there is no necessity of service, because everyone is full. There is no hunger, there is no necessity of eating, but still everyone offers nice things to eat. This is the transcendental world. Unless we attain the stage of simply serving Kṛṣṇa or His devotee, we cannot relish the transcendental pleasure of service. If we have any motive, then that sense will never be awakened. Without a motive, without desire for personal sense gratification, service should be rendered to the Supreme Lord and His devotees.

Do all religions talk about the same perfection?

The purpose of all Vedic instructions is to achieve the ultimate goal of life – to go back to Godhead. All scriptures from all countries aim at this goal. This has also been the message of all religious reformers or teachers. In the West, for example, Lord Jesus Christ spread this same message. Similarly, Lord Buddha and Muhammad. No one advises us to make our permanent settlement here in this material world. There may be small differences according to country, time, circumstance and to scriptural injunction, but the main principle that we are not meant for this material world but for the spiritual world is accepted by all genuine transcendentalists. All indications for the satisfaction of our soul's innermost desires point to those worlds of Kṛṣṇa beyond birth and death.

What is the best service to humanity?

Kṛṣṇa is very much anxious to take us back home, back to Godhead, but we are stubborn and do not wish to go. Therefore He is always looking for the opportunity to take us back home. He is just like an affectionate father. When a son who is a rascal leaves his father and goes loitering in the street with no food and no shelter and suffers very much, the father is always anxious to bring the boy back home. Similarly, Kṛṣṇa is the supreme father, and all the living entities within this material world are exactly like misled children of a wealthy man who have left home to loiter in the street. Therefore the greatest benefit one can bestow on one's fellow human being is to give him Kṛṣṇa consciousness. No kind of material profit will satisfy the living entity, but if he is given Kṛṣṇa consciousness he will actually be satisfied. A bewildered boy loitering in the street may be reminded, 'My dear boy, why are you suffering so much? You are the son of a very rich man who has so much property. Why are you loitering in the street?' And if he comes to understand, 'Yes, I am the son of this important man. Why shall I loiter in the street?' he may then return home. Therefore the best service is to inform those who have forgotten Kṛṣṇa, 'You are part and parcel of Kṛṣṇa. You are the son of Kṛṣṇa, who is full in all opulence. Why are you rotting in this material world?' This is the greatest service.

9

Essays

Teachings of the Vedas

Originally delivered as a lecture on October 6, 1969, at Conway Hall, London, England.

Ladies and gentlemen, today's subject matter is the teachings of the *Vedas*. What are the *Vedas*? The Sanskrit verbal root of *veda* can be interpreted variously, but the purport is finally one. *Veda* means 'knowledge'. Any knowledge you accept is *veda*, for the teachings of the *Vedas* are the original knowledge.

In the conditioned state, our knowledge is subjected to many deficiencies. The difference between a conditioned soul and a liberated soul is that the conditioned soul has four kinds of defects.

The first defect is that he must commit mistakes. For example, in our country, Mahatma Gandhi was considered to be a very great personality, but he committed many mistakes. Even at the last stage of his life, his assistant warned, 'Mahatma Gandhi, don't go to the New Delhi meeting. I have some friends, and I have heard there is danger.' But he did not hear. He persisted in going and was killed. Even great personalities like Mahatma Gandhi, President Kennedy – there are so many of them – make mistakes. To err is human. This is one defect of the conditioned soul.

Another defect: to be illusioned. Illusion means to accept something which is not: *māyā*. *Māyā* means 'what is not'. Everyone is accepting the body as the self. If I ask you what you are, you will say, 'I am Mr. John; I am a rich man; I am this; I am that.' All these are bodily identifications. But you are not this body. This is illusion.

The third defect is the cheating propensity. Everyone has the propensity to cheat others. Although a person is fool number one, he poses himself as very intelligent. Although it is already pointed out that he is in illusion and makes mistakes, he will theorise: 'I think this is this, this is this.' But he does not even know his own position. He writes books of philosophy, although he is defective. That is his disease. That is cheating.

Lastly, our senses are imperfect. We are very proud of our eyes. Often, someone will challenge, 'Can you show me God?' But do you have the eyes to see God? You will never see if you haven't the eyes. If immediately the room becomes dark, you cannot even see your hands. So what power do you have to see? We cannot, therefore, expect knowledge (*veda*) with these imperfect senses. With all these deficiencies, in conditioned life we cannot give perfect knowledge to anyone. Nor are we ourselves perfect. Therefore we accept the *Vedas* as they are.

You may call the *Vedas* Hindu, but 'Hindu' is a foreign name. We are not Hindus. Our real identification is *varṇāśrama. Varṇāśrama* denotes the followers of the *Vedas,* those who accept the human society in eight divisions of *varṇa* and *āśrama.* There are four divisions of society and four divisions of spiritual life. This is called *varṇāśrama.* It is stated in the *Bhagavad-gītā* (4.13), 'These divisions are everywhere because they are created by God.' The divisions of society are *brāhmaṇa, kṣatriya, vaiśya, śūdra. Brāhmaṇa* refers to the very intelligent class of men, those who know what is Brahman. Similarly, the *kṣatriyas,* the administrator group, are the next intelligent class of men. Then the *vaiśyas,* the mercantile group. These natural classifications are found everywhere. This is the Vedic principle, and we accept it. Vedic principles are accepted as axiomatic truth, for there cannot be any mistake. That is acceptance. For instance, in India cow dung is accepted as pure, and yet cow dung is the stool of an animal. In one place you'll find the Vedic injunction that if you touch stool, you have to take a bath immediately. But in another place it is said that the stool of a cow is pure. If you smear cow dung in an impure place, that place becomes pure. With our ordinary sense we can argue, 'This is contradictory.' Actually, it is contradictory from the ordinary point of view, but it is not false. It is fact. In Calcutta, a very prominent scientist and doctor analysed cow dung and found that it contains all antiseptic properties.

In India if one person tells another, 'You must do this', the other party may say, 'What do you mean? Is this a Vedic injunction, that I have to follow you without any argument?' Vedic injunctions cannot be interpreted. But ultimately, if you carefully study why these injunctions are there, you will find that they are all correct.

The *Vedas* are not compilations of human knowledge. Vedic knowledge comes from the spiritual world, from Lord Kṛṣṇa. Another name for the *Vedas* is *śruti. Śruti* refers to that knowledge which is acquired by hearing. It is not experimental knowledge. *Śruti* is considered to be like a mother. We take so much knowledge from our mother. For example, if you want to know who your father is, who can answer you? Your mother. If the mother says, 'Here is your father', you have to accept it. It is not possible to experiment to find out whether he is your father. Similarly, if you want to know something beyond your experience, beyond your experimental knowledge, beyond the activities of the senses, then you have to accept the *Vedas.* There is no question of experimenting. It has already been experimented. It is already settled. The version of the mother, for instance, has to be accepted as truth. There is no other way.

The *Vedas* are considered to be the mother and Brahmā is called the grandfather, the forefather, because he was the first to be instructed in the Vedic knowledge. In the beginning the first living creature was Brahmā. He received this Vedic knowledge and imparted it to Nārada and other disciples and sons, and they also distributed it to their disciples. In this way, the Vedic knowledge comes down by disciplic succession. It is also confirmed in the *Bhagavad-gītā* that Vedic knowledge is understood in this way. If you make experimental endeavour, you come to the same conclusion, but just to save time you should accept. If you want to know who your father is and if you accept your mother as the authority, then whatever she says can be accepted without argument. There are three kinds of evidence: *pratyakṣa, anumāna* and *śabda. Pratyakṣa* means 'direct evidence'. Direct evidence is not very good because our senses are not perfect. We are seeing the sun daily, and it appears to us just like a small disc, but it is actually far, far larger than many planets. Of what value is this seeing? Therefore we have to read books; then we can understand about the sun. So direct experience is not perfect. Then there is *anumāna,* inductive knowledge: 'It may be like this' – hypothesis. For instance, Darwin's theory says it may be like this, it may be like that. But that is not science. That is a suggestion, and it is also not perfect. But if you receive the knowledge from the authoritative sources, that is perfect. If you receive a program guide from the radio station authorities, you accept it. You don't deny it; you don't have to make an experiment, because it is received from the authoritative sources.

Vedic knowledge is called *śabda-pramāṇa.* Another name is *śruti. Śruti* means that this knowledge has to be received simply by aural reception. The *Vedas* instruct that in order to understand transcendental knowledge, we have to hear from the authority. Transcendental knowledge is knowledge from beyond this universe. Within this universe is material knowledge, and beyond this universe is transcendental knowledge. We cannot even go to the end of the universe, so how can we go to the spiritual world? Thus to acquire full knowledge is impossible.

There is a spiritual sky. There is another nature, which is beyond manifestation and nonmanifestation. But how will you know that there is a sky where the planets and inhabitants are eternal? All this knowledge is there, but how will you make experiments? It is not possible. Therefore you have to take the assistance of the *Vedas.* This is called Vedic knowledge. In our Kṛṣṇa consciousness movement we are accepting knowledge from the highest authority, Kṛṣṇa. Kṛṣṇa is accepted as the highest authority by all classes of men. I am speaking first of the two classes of transcendentalists. One class of transcendentalists is called impersonalistic, Māyāvādī. They are generally known as Vedāntists, led by Śaṅkarācārya. And there is another class of transcendentalists, called Vaiṣṇavas, like Rāmānujācārya, Madhvācārya, Viṣṇu Svāmī. Both the Śaṅkara-*sampradāya* and the Vaiṣṇava-*sampradāya* have accepted Kṛṣṇa as the Supreme Personality of Godhead. Śaṅkarācārya is supposed to be an impersonalist who preached impersonalism, impersonal Brahman, but it is a fact that he is a covered personalist. In his commentary on the *Bhagavad-gītā* he wrote, 'Nārāyaṇa, the Supreme Personality of Godhead, is beyond this cosmic manifestation.' And then again he confirmed, 'That Supreme Personality of Godhead, Nārāyaṇa, is Kṛṣṇa. He has come as the son of Devakī and Vasudeva.' He particularly mentioned the names of His father and mother. So Kṛṣṇa is accepted as the Supreme Personality of Godhead by all transcendentalists. There is no doubt about it. Our source of knowledge in Kṛṣṇa consciousness is the *Bhagavad-gītā,* which comes directly from Kṛṣṇa. We have published *Bhagavad-gītā As It Is* because we accept Kṛṣṇa as He is speaking, without any interpretation. That is Vedic knowledge. Since the Vedic knowledge is pure, we accept it. Whatever Kṛṣṇa says, we accept. This is Kṛṣṇa consciousness. That saves much time. If you accept the right authority, or source of knowledge, then you save much time. For example, there are two systems of knowledge in the material world: inductive and deductive. From deductive, you accept that man is mortal. Your father says man is mortal, your sister says man is mortal, everyone says man is mortal – but you do not experiment. You accept it as a fact that man is mortal. If you want to research to find out whether man is mortal, you have to study each and every man, and you may come to think that there may be some man who is not dying but you have not seen him yet. So in this way your research will never be finished. In Sanskrit this process is called *āroha,* the ascending process. If you want to attain knowledge by any personal endeavour, by exercising your imperfect senses, you will never come to the right conclusions. That is not possible.

There is a statement in the *Brahma-saṁhitā:* Just ride on the airplane which runs at the speed of mind. Our material airplanes can run two thousand miles per hour, but what is the speed of mind? You are sitting at home, you immediately think of India – say, ten thousand miles away – and at once it is in your home. Your mind has gone there. The mind-speed is so swift. Therefore it is stated, 'If you travel at this speed for millions of years, you'll find that the spiritual sky is unlimited.' It is not possible even to approach it. Therefore, the Vedic injunction is that one must approach – the word 'compulsory' is used – a bona fide spiritual master, a guru. And what is the qualification of a spiritual master? He is one who has rightly heard the Vedic message from the right source. And he must practically be firmly established in Brahman. These are the two qualities he must have. Otherwise he is not bona fide.

This Kṛṣṇa consciousness movement is completely authorized from Vedic principles. In the *Bhagavad-gītā* Kṛṣṇa says, 'The actual aim of Vedic research is to find out Kṛṣṇa.' In the *Brahma-saṁhitā* it is also stated, 'Kṛṣṇa, Govinda, has innumerable forms, but they are all one.' They are not like our forms, which are fallible. His form is infallible. My form has a beginning, but His form has no beginning. It is *ananta.* And His form – so many multiforms – has no end. My form is sitting here and not in my apartment. You are sitting there and not in your apartment. But Kṛṣṇa can be everywhere at one time. He can sit down in Goloka Vṛndāvana, and at the same time He is everywhere, all-pervading. He is original, the oldest, but whenever you look at a picture of Kṛṣṇa you'll find a young boy fifteen or twenty years old. You will never find an old man. You have seen pictures of Kṛṣṇa as a charioteer from the *Bhagavad-gītā*. At that time He was not less than one hundred years old. He had great-grandchildren, but He looked just like a boy. Kṛṣṇa, God, never becomes old. That is His supreme power. And if you want to search out Kṛṣṇa by studying the Vedic literature, then you will be baffled. It may be possible, but it is very difficult. But you can very easily learn about Him from His devotee. His devotee can deliver Him to you: 'Here He is, take Him.' That is the potency of Kṛṣṇa's devotees.

Originally there was only one *Veda,* and there was no necessity of reading it. People were so intelligent and had such sharp memories that by once hearing from the lips of the spiritual master they would understand. They would immediately grasp the whole purport. But five thousand years ago Vyāsadeva put the *Vedas* in writing for the people in this age, Kali-yuga. He knew that eventually the people would be short-lived, their memories would be very poor and their intelligence would not be very sharp. 'Therefore, let me teach this Vedic knowledge in writing.' He divided the *Vedas* into four: *Ṛg, Sāma, Atharva and Yajur.* Then he gave the charge of these *Vedas* to his different disciples. He then thought of the less intelligent class of men – *strī, śūdra and dvija-bandhu.* He considered the woman class and *śūdra* class (worker class) and *dvija-bandhu. Dvija-bandhu* refers to those who are born in a high family but who are not properly qualified.

A man who is born in the family of a *brāhmaṇa* but is not qualified as a *brāhmaṇa* is called *dvija-bandhu.* For these persons he compiled the *Mahābhārata,* called the history of India, and the eighteen *Purāṇas.*

These are all part of the Vedic literature: the *Purāṇas,* the *Mahābhārata,* the four *Vedas,* and the *Upaniṣads.* The *Upaniṣads* are part of the *Vedas.* Then Vyāsadeva summarised all Vedic knowledge for scholars and philosophers in what is called the *Vedānta-sūtra.* This is the last word of the *Vedas.*

Vyāsadeva personally wrote the *Vedānta-sūtra* under the instructions of Nārada, his Guru Mahārāja (spiritual master), but still he was not satisfied. That is a long story, described in *Śrīmad-Bhāgavatam.* Vedavyāsa was not very satisfied even after compiling many *Purāṇas* and *Upaniṣads,* and even after writing the *Vedānta-sūtra.* Then his spiritual master, Nārada, instructed him, 'You explain the *Vedānta-sūtra.*' *Vedānta* means 'ultimate knowledge', and the ultimate knowledge is Kṛṣṇa. Kṛṣṇa says that throughout all the *Vedas* one has to understand Him: *vedaiś ca sarvair aham eva vedyaḥ.* Kṛṣṇa also says, *vedānta-kṛd veda-vid eva cāham:* 'I am the compiler of the *Vedānta-sūtra,* and I am the knower of the *Vedas.*' Therefore the ultimate objective is Kṛṣṇa. That is explained in all the Vaiṣṇava commentaries on *Vedānta* philosophy. We Gauḍīya Vaiṣṇavas have our commentary on *Vedānta* philosophy, called *Govinda-bhāṣya,* by Baladeva Vidyābhūṣaṇa. Similarly, Rāmānujācārya has a commentary, and Madhvācārya has one. The version of Śaṅkarācārya is not the only commentary. There are many *Vedānta* commentaries, but because the Vaiṣṇavas did not present the first *Vedānta* commentary, people are under the wrong impression that Śaṅkarācārya's is the only *Vedānta* commentary. Besides that, Vyāsadeva himself wrote the perfect *Vedānta* commentary, *Śrīmad-Bhāgavatam. Śrīmad-Bhāgavatam* begins with the first words of the *Vedānta-sūtra: janmādy asya yataḥ.* And that *janmādy asya yataḥ* is fully explained in *Śrīmad-Bhāgavatam.* The *Vedānta-sūtra* simply hints at what is Brahman, the Absolute Truth: 'The Absolute Truth is that from whom everything emanates.' This is a summary, but it is explained in detail in *Śrīmad-Bhāgavatam.* If everything is emanating from the Absolute Truth, then what is the nature of the Absolute Truth? That is explained in *Śrīmad-Bhāgavatam.* The Absolute Truth must be consciousness. He is self-effulgent (*sva-rāṭ*). We develop our consciousness and knowledge by receiving knowledge from others, but for Him it is said that He is self-effulgent. The whole summary of Vedic knowledge is the *Vedānta-sūtra,* and the *Vedānta-sūtra* is explained by the writer himself in *Śrīmad-Bhāgavatam.* We finally request those who are actually after Vedic knowledge to try to understand the explanation of all Vedic knowledge from *Śrīmad-Bhāgavatam* and the *Bhagavad-gītā.*

What Is Kṛṣṇa Consciousness, or Bhakti-yoga?

Bhakti means 'devotional service'. Every service has some attractive feature that drives the servitor progressively on and on. Every one of us in this world is perpetually engaged in some sort of service, and the impetus for such service is the pleasure we derive from it. Driven by affection for his wife and children, a family man works day and night. A philanthropist works in the same way for love of the greater family, and a nationalist for the cause of his country and countrymen. That force that drives the philanthropist, the householder and the nationalist is called *rasa,* or a kind of mellow (relationship) whose taste is very sweet.

Bhakti-rasa is a mellow different from the ordinary *rasa* enjoyed by mundane workers. Mundane workers labour very hard day and night in order to relish a certain kind of *rasa,* which is understood as sense gratification. The relish or taste of the mundane *rasa* does not long endure, and therefore mundane workers are always apt to change their position of enjoyment. A businessman is not satisfied by working the whole week; therefore, wanting a change for the weekend, he goes to a place where he tries to forget his business activities. Then, after the weekend is spent in forgetfulness, he again changes his position and resumes his actual business activities.

Material engagement means accepting a particular status for some time and then changing it. This position of changing back and forth is technically known as *bhoga-tyāga,* which means a position of alternating sense enjoyment and renunciation. A living entity cannot steadily remain either in sense enjoyment or in renunciation. Change is going on perpetually, and we cannot be happy in either state, because of our eternal constitutional position. Sense gratification does not endure for long, and it is therefore called *capala-sukha,* or flickering happiness.

For example, an ordinary family man who works very hard day and night and is successful in giving comforts to the members of his family thereby relishes a kind of mellow, but his whole advancement of material happiness immediately terminates along with his body as soon as his life is over. Death is therefore taken as the representative of God for the atheistic class of men. The devotee realizes the presence of God by devotional service, whereas the atheist realizes the presence of God in the shape of death. At death everything is finished, and one has to begin a new chapter of life in a new situation, perhaps higher or lower than the last one. In any field of activity – political, social, national or international – the result of our actions will be finished with the end of life. That is sure.

Bhakti-rasa, however, the mellow relished in the transcendental loving service of the Lord, does not finish with the end of life. It continues perpetually and is therefore called *amṛta,* that which does not die but exists eternally. This is confirmed in all Vedic literatures. The *Bhagavad-gītā* says that a little advancement in *bhakti-rasa* can save the devotee from the greatest danger – that of missing the opportunity for human life. The *rasas* derived from our feelings in social life, in family life or in the greater family life of altruism, philanthropy, nationalism, socialism, communism, etc., do not guarantee that one's next life will be as a human being.

We prepare our next life by our actual activities in the present life. A living entity is offered a particular type of body as a result of his action in the present body. These activities are taken into account by a superior authority known as *daiva,* or the authority of God. This *daiva* is explained in the *Bhagavad-gītā* as the prime cause of everything, and in *Śrīmad-Bhāgavatam* it is stated that a man takes his next body by *daiva-netreṇa,* which means by the supervision of the authority of the Supreme.

In an ordinary sense, *daiva* is explained as destiny. *Daiva* supervision gives us a body selected from 8,400,000 forms; the choice does not depend on our selection but is awarded to each of us according to our destiny. If our body at present is engaged in the activities of Kṛṣṇa consciousness, then it is guaranteed that we will have at least a human body in our next life. A human being engaged in Kṛṣṇa consciousness, even if unable to complete the course of bhakti-yoga, takes birth in the higher divisions of human society so that he can automatically further his advancement in Kṛṣṇa consciousness. Therefore, all bona fide activities in Kṛṣṇa consciousness are *amṛta,* or permanent.

This eternal engagement in *bhakti-rasa* can be understood by a serious student. Adoption of *bhakti-rasa,* or Kṛṣṇa consciousness, will immediately bring one to an auspicious life free from anxieties and will bless one with transcendental existence, thus minimising the value of liberation. *Bhakti-rasa* itself is sufficient to produce a feeling of liberation, because it attracts the attention of the Supreme Lord, Kṛṣṇa. Generally, neophyte devotees are anxious to see Kṛṣṇa, or God, but God cannot be seen or known by our present materially blunt senses. The process of devotional service as it is recommended in the Vedic literature will gradually elevate one from the material condition of life to the spiritual status, wherein the devotee becomes purified of all designations. The senses can then become uncontaminated, being constantly in touch with *bhakti-rasa.* When the purified senses are employed in the service of the Lord, one becomes situated in *bhakti-rasa* life, and any action performed for the satisfaction of Kṛṣṇa in this transcendental *bhakti-rasa* stage of life can be relished perpetually. When one is thus engaged in devotional service, all varieties of *rasas,* or mellows, turn into eternity. In the beginning one is trained according to the principles of regulation under the guidance of the *ācārya,* or spiritual master, and gradually, when one is elevated, devotional service becomes automatic and spontaneous eagerness to serve Kṛṣṇa. There are twelve kinds of *rasas,* and by renovating our relationship with Kṛṣṇa in five primary *rasas* we can live eternally in full knowledge and bliss.

The basic principle of the living condition is that we have a general propensity to love someone. No one can live without loving someone else. This propensity is present in every living being. Even an animal like a tiger has this loving propensity at least in a dormant stage, and it is certainly present in the human beings. The missing point, however, is where to repose our love so that everyone can become happy. At the present moment the human society teaches one to love his country or family, or his personal self, but there is no information where to repose the loving propensity so that everyone can become happy. That missing point is Kṛṣṇa, and we can learn how to stimulate our original love for Kṛṣṇa and how to be situated in that position where we can enjoy our blissful life.

In the primary stage a child loves his parents, then his brothers and sisters, and as he daily grows up he begins to love his family, society, community, country, nation or even the whole human society. But the loving propensity is not satisfied even by loving all human society; that loving propensity remains imperfectly fulfilled until we know who is the supreme beloved. Our love can be fully satisfied only when it is reposed in Kṛṣṇa.

Our loving propensity expands just as a vibration of light or air expands, but we do not know where it ends. Practising bhakti-yoga teaches us the science of loving every one of the living entities perfectly by the easy method of loving Kṛṣṇa. We have failed to create peace and harmony in human society, even by such great attempts as the United Nations, because we do not know the right method. The method is very simple, but one has to understand it with a cool head. Loving Kṛṣṇa, the Supreme Personality of Godhead, is simple and natural. If we learn how to love Kṛṣṇa, then it is very easy to immediately and simultaneously love every living being. It is like pouring water on the root of a tree or supplying food to one's stomach. The method of pouring water on the root of a tree or supplying foodstuffs to the stomach is universally scientific and practical, as every one of us has experienced. Everyone knows well that when we eat something, or in other words, when we put foodstuffs in the stomach, the energy created by such action is immediately distributed throughout the whole body. Similarly, when we pour water on the root, the energy thus created is immediately distributed throughout the entirety of even the largest tree. It is not possible to water the tree part by part, nor is it possible to feed the different parts of the body separately. Bhakti-yoga will teach us how to turn the one switch that will immediately brighten everything, everywhere. One who does not know this method is missing the point of life.

As far as material necessities are concerned, the human civilization at the present moment is very much advanced in living comfortably, but still we are not happy, because we are missing the point. The material comforts of life alone are not sufficient to make us happy. The vivid example is America: the richest nation of the world, having all facilities for material comfort, is producing a class of men completely confused and frustrated in life. I am appealing herewith to such confused men to learn the art of devotional service, and I am sure that the fire of material existence burning within their hearts will be immediately extinguished. The root cause of our dissatisfaction is that our dormant loving propensity has not been fulfilled despite our great advancement in the materialistic way of life. Bhakti-yoga does not condemn any way of materialistic life, but the attempt is to give information to religionists, philosophers and people in general how to

Who Is Kṛṣṇa?

In the Western countries, whenever someone sees a picture of Kṛṣṇa he immediately asks, 'Who is Kṛṣṇa?' The immediate answer is that Kṛṣṇa is the Supreme Personality of Godhead. How is that? Because He conforms in exact detail to descriptions of the Supreme Being, the Godhead. In other words, Kṛṣṇa is the Godhead because He is all-attractive. Outside the principle of all-attraction, there is no meaning to the word 'Godhead'. How is it one can be all-attractive? First of all, if one is very wealthy, if he has great riches, he becomes attractive to the people in general. Similarly, if someone is very powerful, he also becomes attractive, and if someone is very famous, he also becomes attractive, and if someone is very beautiful or wise or unattached to all kinds of possessions, he also becomes attractive. So from practical experience we can observe that one is attractive due to (1) wealth, (2) power, (3) fame, (4) beauty, (5) wisdom and (6) renunciation. One who is in possession of all six of these opulences at the same time, who possesses them to an unlimited degree, is understood to be the Supreme Personality of Godhead. These opulences of the Godhead are delineated by Parāśara Muni, a great Vedic authority.

We have seen many rich persons, many powerful persons, many famous persons, many beautiful persons, many learned and scholarly persons, and persons in the renounced order of life unattached to material possessions. But we have never seen any one person who is unlimitedly and simultaneously wealthy, powerful, famous, beautiful, wise and unattached, like Kṛṣṇa, in the history of humanity. Kṛṣṇa, the Supreme Personality of Godhead, is a historical person who appeared on this earth 5,000 years ago. He stayed on this earth for 125 years and played exactly like a human being, but His activities were unparalleled. From the very moment of His appearance to the moment of His disappearance, every one of His activities is unparalleled in the history of the world, and therefore anyone who knows what we mean by Godhead will accept Kṛṣṇa as the Supreme Personality of Godhead. No one is equal to the Godhead, and no one is greater than Him. That is the import of the familiar saying 'God is great'.

There are various classes of men in the world who speak of God in different ways, but according to the Vedic literature and according to the great *ācāryas,* the authorized persons versed in the knowledge of God in all ages, like *ācāryas* Śaṅkara, Rāmānuja, Madhva, Viṣṇu Svāmī, Lord Caitanya and all their followers by disciplic succession, all unanimously agree that Kṛṣṇa is the Supreme Personality of Godhead. As far as we, the followers of Vedic civilization, are concerned, we accept the Vedic history of the whole universe, which consists of different planetary systems, called Svargaloka, or the higher planetary system, Martyaloka, or the intermediary planetary system, and Pātālaloka, or the lower planetary system. The modern historians of this earth cannot supply historical evidences of events that occurred before 5,000 years ago, and the anthropologists say that 40,000 years ago Homo sapiens had not appeared on this planet because evolution had not reached that point. But the Vedic histories, such as the *Purāṇas* and *Mahābhārata,* relate human histories that extend millions and billions of years into the past.

For example, from these literatures we are given the histories of Kṛṣṇa's appearances and disappearances millions and billions of years ago. In the fourth chapter of the *Bhagavad-gītā* Kṛṣṇa tells Arjuna that both He and Arjuna had had many births before and that He (Kṛṣṇa) could remember all of them but Arjuna could not. This illustrates the difference between the knowledge of Kṛṣṇa and that of Arjuna. Arjuna might have been a very great warrior, a well-cultured member of the Kuru dynasty, but after all, he was an ordinary human being, whereas Kṛṣṇa, the Supreme Personality of Godhead, is the possessor of unlimited knowledge. Because He possesses unlimited knowledge, Kṛṣṇa has a memory that is boundless.

The knowledge Kṛṣṇa possesses is so perfect that He remembers all the incidents of His appearances some millions and billions of years in the past, but Arjuna's memory and knowledge are limited by time and space, for he is an ordinary human being. In the fourth chapter Kṛṣṇa states that He can remember instructing the lessons of the *Bhagavad-gītā* some millions of years ago to the sun god, Vivasvān.

Nowadays it is the fashion of the atheistic class of men to try to become God by following some mystic process. Generally the atheists claim to be God by dint of their imagination or their meditational prowess. Kṛṣṇa is not that kind of God. He does not become God by manufacturing some mystic process of meditation, nor does He become God by undergoing the severe austerities of the mystic yogic exercises. Properly speaking, He never becomes God because He is the Godhead in all circumstances.

Within the prison of His maternal uncle Kaṁsa, where His father and mother were confined, Kṛṣṇa appeared outside His mother's body as the four-handed Viṣṇu-Nārāyaṇa. Then He turned Himself into a baby and told His father to carry Him to the house of Nanda Mahārāja and his wife Yaśodā. When Kṛṣṇa was just a small baby, the gigantic demoness Pūtanā attempted to kill Him, but when He sucked her breast He pulled out her life. That is the difference between the real Godhead and a God manufactured in the mystic factory. Kṛṣṇa had no chance to practise the mystic yoga process, yet He manifested Himself as the Supreme Personality of Godhead at every step, from infancy to childhood, from childhood to boyhood and from boyhood to young manhood. Although Kṛṣṇa plays like a human being, He always maintains His identity as the Supreme Personality of Godhead.

Since Kṛṣṇa is all-attractive, one should know that all his desires should be focused on Kṛṣṇa. In the *Bhagavad-gītā* it is said that the individual person is the proprietor or master of his own body but that Kṛṣṇa, who is the Supersoul present in everyone's heart, is the supreme proprietor and supreme master of each and every individual body. As such, if we concentrate our loving propensities upon Kṛṣṇa only, then immediately universal love, unity, and tranquillity will be automatically realized. When one waters the root of a tree, he automatically waters the branches, twigs, leaves and flowers; when one supplies food to the stomach through the mouth, he satisfies all the various parts of the body.

The art of focusing one's attention on the Supreme and giving one's love to Him is called Kṛṣṇa consciousness. We have inaugurated the Kṛṣṇa consciousness movement so that everyone can satisfy their propensity for loving others simply by directing their love toward Kṛṣṇa. The whole world is very eager to satisfy the dormant propensity of love for others, but the various invented methods like socialism, communism, altruism, humanitarianism and nationalism, along with whatever else may be manufactured for the peace and prosperity of the world, are all useless and frustrating because of our gross ignorance of the art of loving Kṛṣṇa. Generally people think that by advancing the cause of moral principles and religious rites they will be happy. Others may think that happiness can be achieved by economic development, and yet others think that simply by sense gratification they will be happy. But the real fact is that people can be happy only by loving Kṛṣṇa.

Kṛṣṇa can perfectly reciprocate one's loving propensities in different relationships called mellows, or *rasas*. Basically there are twelve loving relationships. One can love Kṛṣṇa as the supreme unknown, as the supreme master, the supreme friend, the supreme child, the supreme lover. These are the five basic loving *rasas*. One can also love Kṛṣṇa indirectly in seven different relationships, which are apparently different from the five primary relationships. All in all, however, if one simply reposes his dormant loving propensity in Kṛṣṇa, then his life becomes successful. This is not a fiction but is a fact that can be realized by practical application. One can directly perceive the effects that love for Kṛṣṇa has on his life.

In the ninth chapter of the *Bhagavad-gītā* this science of Kṛṣṇa consciousness is called the king of all knowledge, the king of all confidential things and the supreme science of transcendental realization. Yet we can directly experience the results of this science of Kṛṣṇa consciousness because it is very easy to practise and is very pleasurable. Whatever percentage of Kṛṣṇa consciousness we can perform will become an eternal asset to our life, for it is imperishable in all circumstances. It has now been actually proved that today's confused and frustrated younger generation in the Western countries can directly perceive the results of channelling the loving propensity towards Kṛṣṇa alone.

It is said that although one executes severe austerities, penances and sacrifices in his life, if he fails to awaken his dormant love for Kṛṣṇa, then all his penances are to be considered useless. On the other hand, if one has awakened his dormant love for Kṛṣṇa, then what is the use in executing austerities and penances unnecessarily?

The Kṛṣṇa consciousness movement is the unique gift of Lord Caitanya to the fallen souls of this age. It is a very simple method that has actually been carried out during the last so many years in the Western countries, and there is no doubt that this movement can satisfy the dormant loving propensities of humanity. It is said in the *Bhagavad-gītā* that even a little effort expended on the path of Kṛṣṇa consciousness can save one from the greatest danger.

The Six Benefits of Practising Bhakti-yoga

There are six positive benefits when one takes to Kṛṣṇa consciousness. The first is that one feels immediate relief from all kinds of material distress. The great *ācārya* Bhaktivinoda Ṭhākura has written a song stating that when we surrender to Kṛṣṇa we are relieved from all kinds of anxiety. This is very simple to understand. Everyone in the material world is full of anxiety. That is the nature of material existence: problems, one after another. So if someone assures us that 'You just depend on me and I will take charge of your problems,' just imagine how much relief we will feel. Still, if it is an ordinary human being offering us his protection, we may doubt his ability to help us because we know the capacity of an ordinary human being. But when God, Kṛṣṇa, says He will take charge of us, then we can feel full relief. Kṛṣṇa is not an ordinary man; He is the all-powerful Supreme Personality of Godhead, the master of all yogic powers and the Absolute Truth. So when He assures us that 'I take charge of you, and I shall deliver you from the reactions to your sinful activities', we can believe Him.

Suffering is caused by our sinful activities. We enjoy the results of our pious activities and suffer the results of the impious. But whether we enjoy or suffer in this material world, suffering is the common factor. The karmic reactions for performing pious activities are birth in a good family, wealth, good education and beauty. So suppose I perform pious activities and get myself these results. But even if I take birth in the family of a king or a very rich man, the suffering of taking birth is the same. As a poor man suffers in his mother's womb, so a rich man suffers. Suffering is the same whether one is rich or poor. Similarly, disease is not less painful for the rich than for the poor. So as long as we live in the material world our suffering and enjoyment are actually on the same level. There is no real difference between them.

But if we take to Kṛṣṇa consciousness, devotional service to Kṛṣṇa, Kṛṣṇa assures us that 'I shall get you released from all kinds of karmic reactions.' And when Kṛṣṇa takes charge of us He gradually educates us in bhakti-yoga, devotional service, so that we may go back to Him. That is real auspiciousness. The so-called auspiciousness of this world – the attainment of wealth, education, beauty and high parentage – is too adulterated with suffering to actually be considered auspicious.

And as our lives become auspicious when we practise devotional service, so do the lives of other living beings. Therefore devotional service is the best welfare work; it creates good for everyone in all parts of the world without discrimination. Political, sociological and humanitarian acts tend to be partial. That is, they are aimed at a certain section of human beings or animals. But chanting the Hare Kṛṣṇa mantra, which is the primary means to awaken the soul's dormant Kṛṣṇa consciousness, can benefit all beings. Even birds, beasts and insects can awaken to their soul's purpose and become liberated from material suffering simply by hearing the mantra.

At the present moment groups of people are engaged in welfare activities to help their society, community or nation. The United Nations is an attempt to help the world. Their representatives have been tackling various problems for years, but they have not been able to create world harmony. The nations have not united. This is because of the limits of national interest. But Kṛṣṇa consciousness can benefit everyone. Everyone can become attracted by Kṛṣṇa and derive the result.

People want peace, but to get peace they must accept God as the supreme enjoyer. We are not the enjoyers. At the present moment all our activities are self-centred. We think everything in the world is meant for our pleasure. This is wrong. Kṛṣṇa is the enjoyer, the supreme leader and our best friend. He is the proprietor of everything. That is Kṛṣṇa consciousness. This idea should be spread all over the world. Then automatically and very easily the nations will unite.

The next benefit is that one feels great happiness in Kṛṣṇa consciousness. Happiness derived from pure devotional service is the highest because it is eternal, whereas happiness derived from material perfection is temporary. There is no way to prevent oneself from falling from material happiness. But practising pure devotional service offers transcendental pleasure. There is a difference between transcendental pleasure and material pleasure. Material pleasure means sense gratification, and transcendental pleasure means satisfying God. Devotees are satisfied when they see that Kṛṣṇa is pleased. Material pleasure means enjoying directly through the senses, and spiritual pleasure is experienced through Kṛṣṇa. If Kṛṣṇa is satisfied, the devotee is satisfied. The leaves and twigs of a tree are satisfied when they serve the tree's root. Kṛṣṇa is the root; He is the origin of everything. Transcendental pleasure means gaining pleasure by serving the root, Kṛṣṇa.

Transcendental pleasure is also free from envy. If I am interested in selfish pleasure, when I see you happy I tend to become unhappy, and if I see you unhappy I become pleased. It is human nature that if someone is put into difficulty others become happy, and when others are happy, someone is envious of their happiness.

Spiritual pleasure is free of this envy. When devotees see that

Kṛṣṇa or others are happy they become happier. That is the nature of those who are experiencing spiritual pleasure. In the spiritual world there is even a competition to please Kṛṣṇa, but that competition is based on giving Kṛṣṇa pleasure and is not caused by envy. Therefore there is no distress in the spiritual world.

But pure devotional service is rarely achieved because it requires the help of someone fully devoted to Kṛṣṇa. Such persons are free of both material desire and material obligation. They have completely taken shelter of Kṛṣṇa, giving up all other duties. And this is the next advantage of practising bhakti-yoga: one can become free of material obligation.

We all have duties and obligations. We must satisfy our family, our country, the animals in our care, other living entities, the demigods and the saints. We read the scripture, but we must acknowledge that we have received the scripture from he who has revealed it. We are indebted to him. We enjoy and use the sunshine so are indebted to the sun god. We use the moon's rays, the air, the water – so many beings help us live in this world, and we cannot live without their gifts. Who is supplying all our necessities? Of course, they are supplied by God, but He supplies them through His universal administrators, the demigods. Therefore the *Vedas* recommend that one perform sacrifices to show gratitude to the demigods. Those sacrifices are ultimately meant to please the master of the demigods, Kṛṣṇa, so when we take to Kṛṣṇa consciousness we become free of the obligation to express gratitude to each being who has helped us. Fulfilling material obligations is like watering the leaves and twigs of a tree, and worshiping Kṛṣṇa is like watering the root. If we don't water the root of the tree we are bound to water each leaf and twig.

The next benefit of practising devotional service is that we become liberated from material consciousness. As a matter of fact, those who have achieved pure devotional service deride even the concept of liberation. Why doesn't a devotee care about liberation? Because as soon as someone has come to practise pure devotion, liberation is already achieved. There is no need to make a separate endeavour to attain it.

Another name for liberation, *mukti,* is *kaivalya* – the idea that the soul can merge into the undifferentiated form of God and lose its identity. But for one who has realized Kṛṣṇa and His transcendental nature, pastimes and love for His devotees, the idea that 'I have become one with the Supreme' reminds one of hell. Rather, the devotee prefers to remain immersed in the happiness of serving Kṛṣṇa and exchanging with Him in love.

The next effect of practising pure devotional service is that Kṛṣṇa consciousness has the power to attract Kṛṣṇa. Actually, practising devotional service is the *only* means to attract Him. Kṛṣṇa is the Supreme Personality of Godhead with full opulence. We cannot draw Him to us with our wealth, reputation, education, beauty, strength or power of renunciation because He is already self-satisfied and full in Himself. He is the reservoir of all these things. What do we have to offer Him? But we offer what we have in Kṛṣṇa's service and we benefit. The *Vedas* give an example: when a person decorates himself and then looks in the mirror, the person in the reflection is also decorated. Similarly, if we please Kṛṣṇa, we too feel pleasure. It is therefore in our interest to practise bhakti-yoga.

But even though Kṛṣṇa doesn't require anything from us, He is always ready to engage in loving pastimes with us. Kṛṣṇa will be happy that we are doing so much for Him. Although He has everything, He is attracted by our sincerity of purpose. My guru used to say, 'Don't try to see Kṛṣṇa. Serve in such a nice way that Kṛṣṇa will want to see you.' When Kṛṣṇa sees us, our mission is perfect. We cannot perceive Kṛṣṇa by our senses, but when we engage those same senses in satisfying Kṛṣṇa, then Kṛṣṇa will see us. And when Kṛṣṇa sees us, our life will be successful.

The sixth benefit is that a person engaged in Kṛṣṇa consciousness can immediately develop all good qualities. This is because chanting the Hare Kṛṣṇa mantra cleanses the heart of material conceptions. The soul is naturally pure, uncontaminated by the material nature. Although we think we are connected to matter, this is simply an illusion or misidentification. Just as oil and water do not mix, but oil may appear to have fallen into water, so the soul does not mix with matter even though it may appear to be situated in the material world. Rather, the soul is cent percent spiritual.

That we misidentify ourselves with our present body and mind is like seeing a dream. Dreams are false. We are separate from the self we see in the dream. Still, while we are dreaming we may believe we are enjoying or suffering. Similarly, when the soul seems to be situated in material consciousness we think we are enjoying or suffering the things in this world. But it is not true. If we change our consciousness we can immediately transfer ourselves to the spiritual platform.

And because the spiritual platform relates to the soul's true nature, the more advanced we become in Kṛṣṇa consciousness the more the soul's original characteristics, which are very pure, become manifest. The factual example is before us. My European and American disciples were addicted to so many nonsense habits, but since they have taken to Kṛṣṇa consciousness they gave them up immediately and without any great endeavour. So pure character and pure qualities manifest when one practises devotional service.

And the opposite is also true: those who do not practise devotional service cannot have any good qualities no matter how well educated they are. We often see that even university-educated people live like animals. Without God consciousness people cannot rise beyond the sphere of the body and mind and are forced to perform only material activities. They are unable to do any actual good in this world.

We also see that those who are practising other forms of yoga remain restless. Many yoga systems teach that if you become silent, you will realize that you are God. This system may be all right for materialistic persons, but how long will they be able to keep silent? Artificially they may sit down to meditate, but immediately after their yogic performance they engage again in illicit sex, gambling, meat-eating and other nonsensical things.

Actually, yoga practice means *yoga indriya-saṁyamaḥ.* The whole *aṣṭāṅga-yoga* process is meant to control the senses. The senses are like serpents. Even by a touch of its tongue a serpent can cause harm. As it is difficult to enchant a snake, so it is difficult to control the senses. But the yoga system is especially meant to control them – and to control the mind. When the mind and senses are controlled, one is then meant to concentrate on Viṣṇu. This is yoga. But practically we see so many students attending yoga classes who are habituated to nonsense habits – illicit sex, intoxication and meat-eating. That kind of yoga cannot help themselves or anyone else.

Rather, one must develop good character through mind and sense control. Those who are engaged in Kṛṣṇa consciousness automatically give up all nonsense habits and develop high character, and one can develop the highest character by becoming a pure devotee of Kṛṣṇa. The conclusion is that no one can truly have any good qualities if he is lacking Kṛṣṇa consciousness.

To experience these six benefits we have to take to devotional service. Then we shall understand Kṛṣṇa because Kṛṣṇa will reveal Himself to us. If we are engaged in Kṛṣṇa's service constantly – *teṣāṁ satata-yuktānāṁ bhajatāṁ prīti-pūrvakam* – then Kṛṣṇa says *dadāmi buddhi-yogaṁ taṁ yena mām upayānti te:* 'I give the understanding by which they can come to Me.' (*Bhagavad-gītā* 10.10) If you have devoted your heart and soul to serving God, Kṛṣṇa, then Kṛṣṇa is within yourself. He'll give you intelligence and purify your heart.

Appendices

How to Practise Bhakti-yoga

Bhakti-yoga, or Kṛṣṇa consciousness, is about filling your days with activities that help you to know and remember yourself and God. Some call bhakti-yoga the 'yoga of love in action', because all real love is characterized by serving the beloved. Serving Kṛṣṇa – or whatever name you use to call the Divine – draws you into a fully aware, loving, reciprocal relationship with Him. That's Kṛṣṇa consciousness.

Practising bhakti-yoga will change your life in profound ways. It will help you understand the difference between matter and spirit, a discernment the *Vedas* consider the very definition of knowledge. You'll learn to spiritualize your possessions and activities by using them in your pursuit of the Absolute Truth. And you'll learn ways to please God, Kṛṣṇa.

How do we know what pleases Kṛṣṇa? Kṛṣṇa states in the *Bhagavad-gītā* that it's best to follow the teachings of a bona fide spiritual master. If you wish to practise bhakti seriously, you will at some point need a teacher realized in its teachings. His Divine Grace A.C. Bhaktivedanta Swami Prabhupāda, founder-*ācārya* of the International Society for Krishna Consciousness (ISKCON), is one such teacher. Studying his translations and commentaries in books like *Bhagavad-gītā As It Is* and *Śrīmad-Bhāgavatam* will help you immensely as you orient yourself to the Kṛṣṇa conscious paradigm. Śrīla Prabhupāda wrote over sixty books. Lots to start with.

The purpose of spiritual knowledge is to bring us closer to God. Kṛṣṇa says in the *Bhagavad-gītā* (18.55), 'I can be known only by devotional service.' Knowledge guides us in our actions. Spiritual knowledge directs us to satisfy the desires of Kṛṣṇa by engaging ourselves practically in His loving service. Without practical application, theoretical knowledge is of little value. Spiritual knowledge is meant to direct all aspects of one's life. Spiritual practice takes focus and work, so try to organize your life in such a way that you can learn and follow Kṛṣṇa's teachings. Do more than is simply convenient; if you're ready to try it, give it your all.

Chanting the Hare Kṛṣṇa mantra

Bhakti-yogis chant the Hare Kṛṣṇa *mahā-mantra.* Mantras are sounds that both protect and free the mind (*man* – 'mind'; *tra* – 'protector, bringing freedom'), and a *mahā-mantra* is a 'great' mantra.

What is it we have to protect or free the mind from? Everything that covers the soul and its dharma. Matter is diverting. Enamoured by it in its myriad forms, we find ourselves lost in temporary identities – our sex, gender, place in our family, nationality, to name just a few. These false, temporary selves are the source of unhappiness. Chanting the *mahā-mantra* can leave us free to pursue lasting happiness because it puts us in touch with the truth about ourselves.

Śrīla Prabhupāda brought the *mahā-mantra* with him to the

West. It's made of sixteen words arranged in a pattern, so it's easy to learn:

Hare Kṛṣṇa, Hare Kṛṣṇa, Kṛṣṇa Kṛṣṇa, Hare Hare
Hare Rāma, Hare Rāma, Rāma Rāma, Hare Hare

These sixteen words are names of both the feminine and masculine aspects of God. *Hare* refers to Kṛṣṇa's internal energy, His feminine *śakti,* or expression of compassion, service and love. *Kṛṣṇa* refers to God as 'the all-attractive'. Imagine the most beautiful flower or person, and then try to imagine what it would look like if it had unlimited beauty. Kṛṣṇa possesses all opulence. How could He not be *kṛṣṇa,* 'all-attractive'?

Rāma is another name of God, meaning 'reservoir and resting place' – you can repose yourself in Him and find rest.

So the *mahā-mantra* is the infinitesimal soul calling to the Infinite and asking for service: 'O energy of the Lord, O Lord, please engage me in Your service.'

The primary practice of bhakti-yoga is meditation on the spiritual sounds contained in this *mahā-mantra.* Śrīla Prabhupāda writes about what we can expect from chanting the *mahā-mantra:* 'Kṛṣṇa consciousness is not an artificial imposition on the mind; this consciousness is the original energy of the living entity. When we hear the transcendental vibration, this consciousness is revived.... This chanting of Hare Kṛṣṇa, Hare Kṛṣṇa, Kṛṣṇa Kṛṣṇa, Hare Hare / Hare Rāma, Hare Rāma, Rāma Rāma, Hare Hare is directly enacted from the spiritual platform, and thus this sound vibration surpasses all lower strata of consciousness – namely sensual, mental and intellectual.'

Kṛṣṇa is fully present in His names. Vedic texts state that there is no other means of spiritual perfection in the present age other than chanting the *mahā-mantra.* Śrī Caitanya, the fifteenth-century *avatāra* of Kṛṣṇa, made this sublime practice of chanting Hare Kṛṣṇa widely available, declaring that anyone can chant at any time, in any place, under any circumstance and without previous experience.

Mantra meditation

Bhakti-yogis chant in two ways: softly, privately, on beads – a practice called *japa* – or singing with others – a practice called *kīrtana.* Both types of chanting are done attentively and intensely, like a child crying for its mother. Whether you whisper the sacred names in *japa* or sing them in *kīrtana,* pronounce them clearly and distinctly, addressing Kṛṣṇa in a prayerful mood. Simply focus on the sound vibration of the mantra and nothing else, and if your mind wanders, bring it back to the mantra.

If you make a daily commitment to chanting, your mind will begin to release the stress that comes from answering the unending demands of the senses. Your heart will become lighter, and you'll feel yourself coming in contact with a part of yourself you may have only glimpsed. You'll also find yourself, gradually, coming in contact with God.

But be patient, too. We often have a romantic idea of meditation – 'I'll escape worldly distraction, access higher planes of peace, and get a spiritual buzz.' Chanting doesn't always work like that. There are good days and harder days. Sometimes we experience the sweet pleasure that comes from the simple and rhythmic repetition of the *mahā-mantra,* and on other days chanting can feel mechanical, monotonous and uninspired. But chanting is a spiritual discipline. Trust that diligent, determined practice will reawaken the innate spiritual joy that comes from communing with God. In the meantime, even before you taste the highest realizations from chanting, you'll feel more happiness and less stress.

How to chant japa

The early morning hours are the most conducive for *japa* meditation because your body is refreshed from sleep and your environment peaceful. It's a time when the mind can easily flow to Kṛṣṇa. If early mornings aren't possible, find another suitable time in the day. Chant at the same time every day, if possible. That regulation will make the mind friendlier.

Japa meditation is best performed on beads, which help us to both count the mantras and increase our concentration.

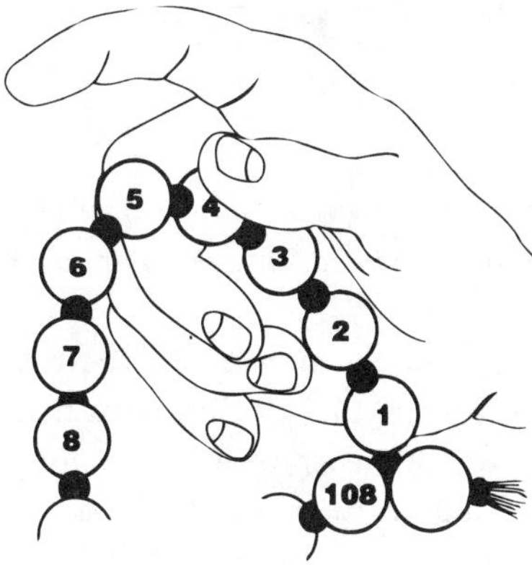

Hold the beads in your right hand, between the thumb and middle finger. Begin chanting one bead to the side of the big centre bead, known as the 'Kṛṣṇa' bead (see diagram). Chant the mantra softly but distinctly, pronouncing it so you can hear it clearly. Then move to the next bead and repeat the mantra. By the time you get back to the Kṛṣṇa bead, you will have chanted the Hare Kṛṣṇa mantra 108 times. This is called 'one round'. Then turn the beads around and start the second round, without crossing over the Kṛṣṇa bead. When you're first starting out, it could take you up to fifteen minutes to chant one round, but with practice, you'll find a round takes only about six or seven minutes.

Start with one round a day and gradually increase. More experienced bhakti-yogis chant between sixteen and sixty-four rounds a day, depending on their vow, schedule and lifestyle. Sixteen rounds takes about two hours. Once you commit to chanting a certain number of rounds daily, try not to go below this number. Consistency is helpful for spiritual progress because it creates mental discipline.

You may find it helpful to begin your *japa* session, or even each round, with the Pañca-tattva mantra – a prayer to Lord Caitanya and His associates. Lord Caitanya's primary mission was to teach bhakti-yoga, and He embodies compassion for all who suffer in the material world.

The mantra is:

śrī-kṛṣṇa-caitanya prabhu-nityānanda
śrī-advaita gadādhara śrīvāsādi-gaura-bhakta-vṛnda

This mantra consists of the names of Śrī Kṛṣṇa Caitanya and His four principal associates – Prabhu Nityānanda, Śrī Advaita, Gadādhara, and Śrīvāsa – each of whom represents a particular devotional understanding. *Gaura-bhakta-vṛnda* means 'all others in the line of devotion'.

How to chant kīrtana

Singing the *mahā-mantra* in *kīrtana* is usually done with others. Singing a mantra barely requires instruction, but *kīrtana* is also mantra meditation, so the same points mentioned in regard to *japa* apply here – concentration on clear pronunciation and hearing the sound of the holy names. *Kīrtana* is traditionally done in a call-and-response fashion to facilitate both hearing the mantra and chanting it.

Since God is all-powerful and all-merciful, He has invested Himself in His names. When we name someone or something in this world – John, Mary, water, tree – we may evoke remembrance of the person or thing, but because the owners of those names are only temporary physical manifestations, their names don't really evoke them on the spiritual level and so have little power. Try chanting 'water, water' and see if your thirst is quenched.

The names of God and God Himself, on the other hand, are identical. This means that when we chant the holy names Hare, Kṛṣṇa and Rāma, we are directly associating with God and His energies and being purified of all unwanted qualities in ourselves that stop us from knowing ourselves. To know ourselves is to know God also.

A melodious *kīrtana* with family or friends is sure to enliven everyone. There are traditional melodies and instruments. If you'd like to hear them, there are hundreds of *kīrtanas* posted online. But feel free to chant to any melody that works and use any musical instruments you like to accompany your chanting.

Eating karma-free

Eating karma-free starts with responsible eating – choosing a violence-free, sustainable, vegetarian diet. In the *Bhagavad-gītā* Kṛṣṇa states, 'If one offers Me with love and devotion a leaf, a flower, fruit or water, I will accept it.' So preparing pure, natural, vegetarian food is the first step. Offering that food back to Kṛṣṇa in a spirit of gratitude and devotion is the second. Offered food is called *prasāda*, 'grace'. *Prasāda* also means 'light' or 'clarity'. So while *prasāda* nourishes the body, it also transforms the consciousness. Think of *prasāda* as a way to immunize yourself against illusion and the kinds of material influences that draw you into an exploitative relationship with the material world.

Śrīla Prabhupāda made honouring *prasāda* a prominent feature of the Hare Kṛṣṇa movement. At the first ISKCON temple, established in a New York City storefront, Śrīla Prabhupāda personally prepared, offered and served sumptuous vegetarian *prasāda* dishes to his young guests. Śrīla Prabhupāda also trained his new disciples in the art of cooking with bhakti. Those lessons included how to be clean in body and mind, how to keep the kitchen clean and how use a variety of grains, fruits, vegetables and spices to create stunning dishes. He repeatedly requested his disciples to preserve what he had taught them, and he stated boldly that we could eat our way to Kṛṣṇa consciousness!

Kṛṣṇa declares in the *Bhagavad-gītā* that He will accept 'a leaf, a flower, fruit or water' if offered with love and devotion. This indicates that He accepts only vegetarian foods. Yoga culture teaches that all life is sacred, and to kill innocent animals unnecessarily is a gross violation of God's laws. Vegetarianism is also an essential step toward creating a better society, and people who take the time to consider its advantages will be in the company of Socrates, Leonardo da Vinci, George Harrison, Mahatma Gandhi, Albert Einstein and a host of contemporary thinkers, artists, musicians, and neighbours. Vegetarianism makes sense in terms of health, economics, ethics and spirituality. It's a natural, healthy, nonviolent way to live, and it awakens our sense of compassion for all those with whom we share the planet.

So let your eating become a sacred, soul-enlivening activity. Spiritualize your food by offering it to Kṛṣṇa with love and devotion. And by the way, when you're shopping, read labels carefully, because many ready-made products contain meat, fish or eggs. When you're preparing a meal, use fresh, natural and wholesome ingredients as often as you can. Cleanliness is also important. Avoid tasting the food while you're cooking – you're making a meal for Kṛṣṇa's pleasure, so let Him be the first taster. For those who may not be experienced in vegetarian cooking, a variety of easy-to-follow recipes can be found in various Hare Kṛṣṇa cookbooks. (Consider starting with *The Higher Taste* – available from Amazon or your local ISKCON temple.)

How to offer food

Reserve a special plate for offerings. Once you've finished cooking, put the food on the plate and place it in front of a picture of

Kṛṣṇa. You can recite the Sanskrit mantras below or simply ask Kṛṣṇa to please accept the offering. The most important part of making an offering is your intention, so try to clear your mind and fix it on what you are about to do.

Start with chanting the Hare Kṛṣṇa mantra three times:

Hare Kṛṣṇa, Hare Kṛṣṇa, Kṛṣṇa Kṛṣṇa, Hare Hare
Hare Rāma, Hare Rāma, Rāma Rāma, Hare Hare

Then, members of the Hare Kṛṣṇa movement recite the following three mantras, also three times each, while making an offering:

nama oṁ viṣṇu-pādāya kṛṣṇa-preṣṭhāya bhū-tale
srīmate bhaktivedānta-svāmin iti nāmine

namas te sārasvate deve gaura-vāṇī-pracāriṇe
nirviśeṣa-śūnyavādi-pāścātya-deśa-tāriṇe

'I offer my respectful obeisances unto His Divine Grace A.C. Bhaktivedanta Swami Prabhupāda, who is very dear to Lord Kṛṣṇa, having taken shelter at His lotus feet. Our respectful obeisances are unto you, O spiritual master, servant of Bhaktisiddhānta Sarasvatī. You are kindly preaching the message of Lord Caitanya and delivering the Western countries, which are filled with impersonalism and voidism.'

This first mantra is to the spiritual master. We learn from our teachers, and the spiritual master teaches the most valuable lessons – who we are and why we are here – and so our spiritual masters are dear to Kṛṣṇa. In humility, we ask to serve by offering our spiritual master what we have cooked and asking him to offer it to Kṛṣṇa.

namo mahā-vadānyāya
kṛṣṇa-prema-pradāya te

kṛṣṇāya kṛṣṇa-caitanya-
nāmne gaura-tviṣe namaḥ

'O most munificent incarnation, You are Kṛṣṇa Himself appearing as Śrī Kṛṣṇa Caitanya Mahāprabhu. You have assumed the golden colour of Śrīmatī Rādhārāṇī, and You are widely distributing pure love of Kṛṣṇa. We offer our respectful obeisances unto You.'

This second mantra invokes Caitanya Mahāprabhu, the compassionate *avatāra* of Kṛṣṇa who distributed love of God through *saṅkīrtana.*

namo brahmaṇya-devāya
go-brāhmaṇa-hitāya ca
jagad-dhitāya kṛṣṇāya
govindāya namo namaḥ

'My Lord, You are the well-wisher of the cows and the *brāhmaṇas,* and You are the well-wisher of the entire human society and the world.'

This third mantra invokes Kṛṣṇa, Govinda, who does good for all.

After offering the food, wait at least five minutes for Kṛṣṇa to accept the preparations. You can then transfer the food from the offering plate to your plate and wash the offering plate.

Now you can serve the *prasāda* to your friends and family. While you eat, try to appreciate the spiritual value of the food. Remember that the real purpose of preparing and offering food to Kṛṣṇa is to show your devotion and gratitude to Him. Kṛṣṇa is attracted by the devotion, love and sincerity in an offering. He is complete in Himself – He doesn't require anything from us – but out of His immense kindness He allows us to offer Him food so we can begin to develop love for Him.

It's not just food that becomes *prasāda* when you offer it. Anything you offer – flowers, incense, water, your work, yourself –

becomes spiritualized as Kṛṣṇa accepts and blesses the offerings. We should, therefore, not only deeply respect the things we've offered but share them with others. Giving others the grace of God is an essential part of bhakti-yoga.

Creating a sacred space

We live in a complex world, and that forces us to complicate our lives just to survive. Most of us live far from the peacefulness of the rural villages of bygone ages, where people moved at a slower pace and spiritual culture was woven into the fabric of everyday life. Where can we go nowadays to reflect? Those looking for a little spiritual respite may like to create a sacred space in their homes.

In Sanskrit, a sacred space is called a *mandira,* literally, a place of 'inward habitation'. *Mandiras* help the mind become steady and peaceful. You can transform your home into such a sanctuary by creating an altar, where you can reflect, refocus and rejuvenate.

Start by keeping your home clean, tidy and uncluttered. That will help keep the mind peaceful. Then find a quiet place in your home where you can set up an altar. Let that area become the spiritual hub of your home, and the place where you chant *japa* and offer your food. It's likely that if you take the trouble to create an altar, you'll find that your *japa* and *kīrtana* are especially easy and effective when you practise them there. Sacred spaces inspire bhakti, especially if you beautify them with meaningful spiritual pictures, fresh flowers, incense and candles. You can visit your altar when you rise in the morning, offer respects to Kṛṣṇa and your teachers there, and express gratitude for all the gifts your life has brought you. You can use that time to align yourself for the day ahead. Food offerings can be placed on the altar. The family can come together there to chant, read sacred texts, or just spend time together talking about Kṛṣṇa. The time you spend at your altar will help you prepare for the world outside your front door, and it will be a place to which you can return for reflection at any time of day.

To set up your altar, use a small table, shelf or mantle, ideally in a clean, well-lit place free from too much household traffic. If you have a separate room you can use, great; if not, simply dedicate whatever space you have to Kṛṣṇa and don't use it for other purposes.

Place pictures of Kṛṣṇa or other sacred images on your altar. Think of Kṛṣṇa as your guest. You wouldn't seat a guest in your home and then ignore him. So place some seats around your altar, too, so you can sit and exchange with Kṛṣṇa and your fellow bhakti-yogis.

A simple altar, Hare Kṛṣṇa style

Essentials:

1. A picture of Śrīla Prabhupāda
2. A picture of Lord Caitanya and His associates
3. A picture of Rādhā and Kṛṣṇa

We begin meditation or worship by respecting the spiritual master. The spiritual master is Kṛṣṇa's dear servant and representative, and we owe him an immense debt of gratitude for the knowledge he gives us about ourselves and our relationship with Kṛṣṇa. Hare Kṛṣṇa devotees place a picture of their guru, Śrīla Prabhupāda, on their altars.

After honouring the guru, we turn our meditation to Śrī Caitanya and His four principal associates – collectively known as the Pañca-tattva ('five truths'). Lord Caitanya is the incarnation of Kṛṣṇa for this age, appearing in the form of a pure bhakti-yogi in order to teach us how to love God. It is Lord Caitanya who first introduced the congregational chanting of the Hare Kṛṣṇa *mahā-mantra* (*saṅkīrtana*).

After respecting Kṛṣṇa in this merciful and compassionate

form, we turn to the Supreme Personality of Godhead, Lord Kṛṣṇa, and His eternal consort, Śrīmatī Rādhārāṇī. Śrīmatī Rādhārāṇī is Kṛṣṇa's female counterpart and His most beloved devotee. It is from Her that we learn how best to serve Kṛṣṇa.

Here's a drawing of how you can arrange these pictures on your altar:

Along with daily offerings of food and water, you can offer incense and fresh flowers. Clean your altar regularly, ideally daily. You wouldn't neglect to clean a guest's room, and when you establish an altar, you are inviting Kṛṣṇa and His pure devotees to live as guests in your home. If you are offering fresh water, rinse the cups and fill them daily. Remove any wilted flowers from vases. Offer incense at least once a day. Consider lighting candles and placing them near the pictures while you're chanting.

Studying sacred texts

In the *Bhagavad-gītā* (4.38) Kṛṣṇa states, 'In this world, there is nothing so sublime and pure as transcendental knowledge.' When

Śrīla Prabhupāda presented and commentated the timeless wisdom of the Vedic texts, he transformed spiritual sound into the printed word and made it readily available to us. Reading sacred texts, such as the *Bhagavad-gītā* or *Śrīmad-Bhāgavatam* (or texts sacred to your own tradition) can infuse you with insight, inspiration and faith. As with chanting, it's best to read daily, noting interesting passages and contemplating their meaning.

Śrīla Prabhupāda taught that while reading sacred texts is essential for those who wish to practise bhakti, it's also important to discuss what one reads with others. Personal study combined with discussion is the best way to assimilate knowledge. In Hare Kṛṣṇa temples around the world there are morning and evening classes in the essential texts of bhakti-yoga. These classes are open to all. There are also a number of courses in bhakti-yoga both for beginners and the more adept.

Practising bhakti-yoga is simple, really – hearing spiritual texts, chanting God's names alone and with family and friends and eating *prasāda.* All of these practices, if done mindfully, will nurture the love for God you already have within you, and they'll also help you realize how much God loves you. Reciprocating with God's love is the essence of bhakti-yoga.

Want more information about anything you've read in this section? Please visit krishnawisdom.com.

Śrīla Prabhupāda

His Divine Grace A.C. Bhaktivedanta Swami Prabhupāda (1896–1977) is widely regarded as the world's preeminent exponent of the teachings and practices of bhakti-yoga in the Western world. Born Abhay Charan De on September 1, 1896, in Calcutta, as a young man he was involved with Mahatma Gandhi's civil disobedience movement. Meeting prominent scholar and spiritual teacher Śrīla Bhaktisiddhānta Sarasvatī Ṭhākura, however, influenced his life's direction. Śrīla Bhaktisiddhānta represented the ancient bhakti tradition, and even at their first meeting he asked Abhay to carry the bhakti teachings to the English-speaking world.

Abhay had been raised in a family devoted to Kṛṣṇa – the name of God meaning 'the all-attractive and all-loving'. Deeply moved by Śrīla Bhaktisiddhānta's devotion and wisdom, Abhay became his disciple and dedicated himself to carrying out his teacher's request, although he wouldn't set out for the West until 1965, when he was almost seventy years old.

In 1965, after being awarded the honorary title of Bhaktivedanta in recognition of his learning and devotion and having taken the vows of a renunciant, Abhay Charan, now known as Bhaktivedanta Swami, begged passage from a local steamship company and travelled as the sole passenger aboard a small, weathered cargo ship named the Jaladuta. In his possession were a suitcase, an umbrella, a supply of dry cereal, about seven dollars' worth of Indian currency and several boxes of books.

The journey proved treacherous, and he suffered two heart attacks on the way. But after thirty-seven days at sea, on September 17 of that year, he arrived at a lonely Brooklyn pier. He had come to America knowing no one, with absolutely no visible means of support, and with only the meagre handful of possessions he had carried on board. He had no money, no friends, no followers; he was elderly, his health was not good, and he had no clear idea of how he would accomplish his far-reaching objective to present the spiritual knowledge of the *Vedas* to the entire Western society.

In a poem written in Bengali just after his arrival, Bhaktivedanta Swami expressed his humble faith in Lord Kṛṣṇa and the special instruction of his own spiritual master, who had intended him to spread the teachings of Kṛṣṇa consciousness throughout the English-speaking world: 'My dear Lord Kṛṣṇa...How will I make them understand this message of Kṛṣṇa consciousness? I am very unfortunate, unqualified, and the most fallen. Therefore I am seeking Your benediction so that I can convince them, for I am powerless to do so on my own.... I am sure that when this transcendental message penetrates their hearts they will certainly feel engladdened and thus become liberated from all unhappy conditions of life.'

This poem was written on September 18, 1965. Just twelve years later, on November 14, 1977, Bhaktivedanta Swami passed away in India at the age of 81. What was Bhaktivedanta Swami able to accomplish during this brief period, having begun with nothing and at an age when most are ready to retire? The list of accomplishments is striking by any standard.

The beginning

'I have come here in this old age neither for sightseeing nor for personal interest. It is for implementing the science of Kṛṣṇa, which will actually make people happy.'

In New York City Śrīla Prabhupāda faced hardships without money or a place to live, and so his mission began humbly. He gave classes on the *Bhagavad-gītā* in a loft on the Bowery, New York's infamous skid row, and led *kīrtana* (traditional devotional chanting) in Tompkins Square Park. His message of peace and goodwill resonated with many young people, some of whom came forward to become serious students of the Kṛṣṇa bhakti tradition. With the help of these students, Bhaktivedanta Swami rented a small storefront on New York's Lower East Side to use as a temple.

In July 1966, Śrīla Prabhupāda established the International Society for Krishna Consciousness 'for the purpose of checking the imbalance of values in the world and working for real unity and peace'. He taught that each soul is part and parcel of the quality of God and that one could find true happiness through living a simpler, more natural way of life and dedicating one's energy to the service of God and all living beings.

Next, Śrīla Prabhupāda travelled to San Francisco where, amidst the emerging hippie community in the Haight-Ashbury district during 1967's 'Summer of Love', he taught that chanting the Hare Kṛṣṇa mantra was a spiritual high superior to any pleasures derived from wealth, fame or the then burgeoning world of intoxication. In the following months many came forward to assist him, and his fledging movement spread to various cities in the United States and Canada. His talks about the importance of developing communities based on 'simple living and high thinking' also inspired a number of his disciples to develop farm communities. As his young followers married and had children, they opened schools.

In 1967, six of his young disciples took the bhakti-yoga movement to London. In the middle of a winter of struggle came a fortunate break for the London devotees: a meeting with George Harrison of the Beatles. The rest, they say, is history, as the Hare Kṛṣṇa mantra went to the top of the pop charts and the movement spread from London to other parts of the UK as well as to most of the major cities of Europe. By 1971 Śrīla Prabhupāda had visited Communist Russia, speaking in his hotel room with a couple of interested guests, who then began the monumental task of sharing Kṛṣṇa consciousness and the *Bhagavad-gītā* he had left them with the people of their country. He also sent followers to Africa that year.

In the eleven years that followed the founding of the International Society for Krishna Consciousness, Śrīla Prabhupāda circled the globe fourteen times, bringing the teachings of bhakti to thousands of people on six continents. Men and women from all backgrounds came forward to learn and practise his teachings. With their help, Śrīla Prabhupāda established centres and projects throughout the world, including temples, rural communities, educational institutions and what would become the world's largest vegetarian food relief program. With the desire to nourish the roots of Kṛṣṇa bhakti in its home, Śrīla Prabhupāda returned to India several times, where he sparked a revival of the bhakti tradition and opened dozens of temples, including important centres in the holy towns of Vṛndāvana and Māyāpur.

ISKCON and its seven purposes

In 1966, when Śrīla Prabhupāda legally established the International Society for Krishna Consciousness (ISKCON), he listed seven purposes in his articles of incorporation. At the time, the movement had few followers in the West and was operating out of a rented storefront in New York City. In the years that followed, Śrīla Prabhupāda expanded ISKCON's mission and activities beyond some of the details listed in the incorporation documents yet remained consistent with their principles. For example, Śrīla Prabhupāda wanted ISKCON to establish 'a holy place of transcendental pastimes dedicated to the personality of Krishna', and ISKCON has since established many such holy places, with temples in major cities around the world. He also wanted 'to bring the members closer together for the purpose of teaching a simpler, more natural way of life', and this has inspired the development of self-sufficient farm communities, ashrams and spiritual retreat centres.

Śrīla Prabhupāda's seventh purpose was this: 'With a view towards achieving the aforementioned purposes, to publish and distribute periodicals, magazines, books and other writings.' Kṛṣṇa consciousness is more than just another sectarian faith; it's a technical science of spiritual values that is fully described in the Vedic literature of ancient India. The aim of the Kṛṣṇa consciousness movement is to acquaint people all over the world with these universal principles of God realization so that they may derive the highest benefits of spiritual understanding, unity and peace.

Śrīla Prabhupāda's books

Śrīla Prabhupāda often described his work of translating and explaining the ancient Vedic texts as the heart of his mission, and during his lifetime he authored over seventy volumes on bhakti-yoga, books that are highly respected for their authority, depth, clarity and fidelity to the tradition. These writings have been translated into more than eighty languages. His most prominent works include *Bhagavad-gītā As It Is,* and the multivolume *Śrīmad-Bhāgavatam* and *Śrī Caitanya-caritāmṛta.*

In 1972, Śrīla Prabhupāda founded the Bhaktivedanta Book Trust, now the world's largest publisher of Vedic literature. Through its work over the last almost fifty years, a number of his books are now available in over eighty languages, and millions of people have read at least one of them. Many have felt their lives genuinely enriched.

The Vedic teachings presented in Śrīla Prabhupāda's books can be summarized under three general headings, known in Sanskrit as *sambandha, abhidheya* and *prayojana. Sambandha* means our relationship with God; *abhidheya* means acting in that relationship; and *prayojana* means the ultimate goal or perfection. These three divisions of understanding represent universal principles common to all the religious teachings of the world.

The knowledge described in Śrīla Prabhupāda's books enables anyone to advance in his or her understanding of God without having to change current religious, national or cultural affiliations. The science of how to understand God, how to understand one's relationship with God and how to develop love for God has nothing to do with sectarian faiths. These are objectives no religion in the world could deny. They are, in other words, the essence of religion – universal features by which all religions may be understood.

Preferences regarding God's holy name may differ from one religion to another, modes of worship may differ, and details of ritual and doctrine may differ as well. But the test is how much the practitioner actually develops knowledge of and love for God. Real religion means to learn to love God. And how to love God is the sum and substance of the teachings found in Śrīla Prabhupāda's books.

Glossary

Ācārya – one who teaches by example.

Arjuna – the third son of Pāṇḍu and an intimate friend of Lord Kṛṣṇa's. Kṛṣṇa became his chariot driver and spoke the *Bhagavad-gītā* to him on the battlefield of Kurukṣetra.

Bhagavad-gītā – a seven-hundred-verse record of a conversation between Lord Kṛṣṇa and His disciple Arjuna, recorded in the *Mahābhārata.*

Bhakti – Pure devotional service to God.

Bhakti-rasa – relationship between God and the living entities; the sweet taste of that relationship.

Bhakti-yoga – the system of cultivation of bhakti. Yoga literally means 'to link', so it is the process of linking with the Supreme through devotional service.

Brahmā – the first created being of the universe and therefore the forefather. He is also the giver of the *Vedas* and the director of the secondary phase of cosmic creation by which all species of plants, animals, human beings and demigods come into existence.

Brahman – The Absolute Truth.

Caitanya-caritāmṛta – the foremost biography of Śrī Caitanya Mahāprabhu. Written in Bengali and Sanskrit in the late sixteenth century by Śrīla Kṛṣṇadāsa Kavirāja Gosvāmī.

Caitanya Mahāprabhu (1486–1534) – Lord Kṛṣṇa appearing as His own devotee. He inaugurated the congregational chanting of the holy names of the Lord (*saṅkīrtana*) to teach pure love of God.

Disciplic succession – a chain of spiritual masters and their disciples who in turn became spiritual masters.

False ego – the conception that 'I am this material body, mind or intelligence.'

Goloka Vṛndāvana – the spiritual world.

Guru – spiritual master.

Liberation – freedom from birth and death.

Mahā-mantra – 'the great mantra': *Hare Kṛṣṇa, Hare Kṛṣṇa, Kṛṣṇa Kṛṣṇa, Hare Hare / Hare Rāma, Hare Rāma, Rāma Rāma, Hare Hare.*

Mantra – a pure sound vibration that when repeated delivers the mind from its material inclinations and illusion. A transcendental sound or Vedic hymn, prayer or chant; Combining the Sanskrit terms *manas* ('mind') and *trayate* ('to deliver'), a mantra is a spiritual sound that frees consciousness from illusion. The Vedic scriptures are composed of thousands of mantras.

Māyā – Illusion; literally, 'that which is not'.

Nārada Muni – a pure devotee of the Lord, one of the sons of Lord Brahmā, who travels throughout the universe in his eternal body teaching the science of bhakti. He is the spiritual master of Vyāsadeva and of many other great devotees.

Rādhā[rāṇī] – Lord Kṛṣṇa's most intimate consort, who personifies His pleasure potency.

Rasa – relationship.

Sampradāya – literally, 'community'; a disciplic succession.

Self-realization – the understanding that one is not the body but a soul and that one is an eternal servant of God.

Śrīmad-Bhāgavatam – the foremost of the eighteen *Purāṇas*. The complete science of God, it establishes the supreme position of Lord Kṛṣṇa.

Vaiṣṇava – a devotee of the Supreme Lord Viṣṇu, or Kṛṣṇa

Varṇāśrama – the Vedic social system, which organizes society into four occupational and four spiritual divisions (*varṇas* and *āśramas*) based on quality of work and situation with regard to the modes of nature (*guṇas*).

Vedānta – the philosophy of the *Vedānta-sūtra* of Śrīla Vyāsadeva, containing a conclusive summary of Vedic philosophical knowledge and showing Kṛṣṇa as the goal.

Vedas – the four original scriptures (*Ṛg, Sāma, Atharva* and *Yajur*).

Guide to Sanskrit Pronunciation

The system of transliteration used in this book conforms to a system that scholars have accepted to indicate the pronunciation of each sound in the Sanskrit language.

The short vowel **a** is pronounced like the **u** in b**u**t, long **ā** like the **a** in f**a**r. Short **i** is pronounced as **i** in p**i**n, long **ī** as in p**i**que, short **u** as in p**u**ll, and long **ū** as in r**u**le. The vowel **ṛ** is pronounced like **ri** in **ri**m, **e** like the **ey** in th**ey**, **o** like the **o** in g**o**, **ai** like the **ai** in **ai**sle, and **au** like the **ow** in h**ow**. The *anusvara* (**ṁ**) is pronounced like the **n** in the French word *bo***n**, and *visarga* (**ḥ**) is pronounced as a final **h** sound. At the end of a couplet, **aḥ** is pronounced **aha**, and **iḥ** is pronounced **ihi**.

The guttural consonants – **k, kh, g, gh** and **ṅ** – are pronounced from the throat in much the same manner as in English. **K** is pronounced as in **k**ite, **kh** as in Ec**kh**art, **g** as in **g**ive, **gh** as in di**g-h**ard, and **ṅ** as in si**ng**.

The palatal consonants – **c, ch, j, jh** and **ñ** – are pronounced with the tongue touching the firm ridge behind the teeth. **C** is pronounced as in **ch**air, **ch** as in staun**ch-h**eart, **j** as in **j**oy, **jh** as in he**dgeh**og, and **ñ** as in ca**ny**on.

The cerebral consonants – **ṭ, ṭh, ḍ, ḍh** and **ṇ** – are pronounced with the tip of the tongue turned up and drawn back against the dome of the palate. **Ṭ** is pronounced as in **t**ub, **ṭh** as in ligh**t-h**eart, **ḍ** as in **d**ove, **ḍh** as in re**d-h**ot, and **ṇ** as in **n**ut.

The dental consonants – **t, th, d, dh** and **n** – are pronounced in the same manner as the cerebrals, but with the forepart of the tongue against the teeth.

The labial consonants – **p, ph, b, bh** and **m** – are pronounced with the lips. **P** is pronounced as in **p**ine, **ph** as in u**ph**ill, **b** as in **b**ird, **bh** as in ru**b-h**ard, and **m** as in **m**other.

The semivowels – **y, r, l** and **v** – are pronounced as in **y**es, **r**un, **l**ight and **v**ine respectively. The sibilants – **ś, ṣ** and **s** – are pronounced, respectively, as in the German word **s***prechen* and the English words **sh**ine and **s**un. The letter **h** is pronounced as in **h**ome.

SELECTED ADDRESSES

International Society for Krishna Consciousness

Founder-*Ācārya*: His Divine Grace A.C. Bhaktivedanta Swami Prabhupāda

Visit **centres.iskcon.org** or **directory.krishna.com** for the unabridged address list. For further information on classes, programmes, festivals, residential courses, and local meetings please contact the centre nearest you. Addresses as of September 2018.

✦ centre with restaurant
✧ restaurant

United Kingdom and Ireland

Hare Krishna meetings are held regularly in more than forty towns in the UK. For more information, visit us on the web at **iskconuk.com** or contact ISKCON Reader Services, P.O. Box 730, Watford, WD25 8ZE; readerservices@pamho.net

Belfast, Northern Ireland – 2a Brooklands Grange, Dunmurry, Belfast, BT17 OHE; +44 28 9062 0530; info@iskconbelfast.co.uk; iskconbelfast.co.uk

Birmingham, England – iskconbirmingham@gmail.com; iskconbirmingham.org

Cardiff, Wales – Ty Krishna Cymru, 4 Dock Chambers, Bute Street, Cardiff, CF10 5AG; +44 29 2019 3346; info@iskconwales.org.uk; iskconwales.org.uk

Coventry, England – Shree Shree Radha Krishna Cultural Centre, Kingfield Road, Radford, West Midlands, Coventry, CV1 4DW; +44 2476 552 822; kov@krishnaofvrindavan.com; krishnaofvrindavan.com

Crawley, England – Bhakti Yoga Centre, Spindle Way, Crawley, RH10 1TG; +44 7862 244554; info@iskconcrawley.co.uk; bhaktiyogacentre.com

Dublin, Ireland ✦ Govinda's Kirtan Centre, 83 Middle Abbey Street, Dublin 1, D01 EV91; +353 87 992 1332; dublin@krishna.ie; mark@govindas.ie; krishna.ie; govindas.ie

Edinburgh, Scotland – +44 7434 030208; iskconedinburgh.com

Folkestone, England – Atma Lounge, 54 The Old High Street, Kent, Folkestone, C20 1RN; +44 1303 243482; info@atmalounge.com; atmalounge.com

Leicester, England – 31 Granby Street, Leicester, LE1 6EJ; +44 7597 786 676; info@iskconleicester.org; iskconleicester.org

London (City), England ✦ Sri Sri Radha-Krishna Temple, 10 Soho Street, London, W1D 3DL; +44 20 7437 3662; +44 20 3687 0617; info@iskcon-london.org; govindas@iskcon-london.org; iskcon-london.org

London (King's Cross), England – Matchless Gifts, 102 Caledonian Road, King's Cross, Islington, London, N1 9DN; +44 20 7168 5732; foodforalluk@gmail.com; matchlessgifts.foodforall.org.uk

London (South), England – 42 Enmore Road, South Norwood, London, SE25 5NG; +44 20 8407 6127; iskcon.southlondon@googlemail.com; iskconsouthlondon.org

Manchester, England – 20 Mayfield Road, Whalley Range, Manchester, M16 8FT; +44 161 226 4416; contact@iskconmanchester.com; iskconmanchester.com

Newcastle-upon-Tyne, England – 304 Westgate Road, Newcastle-upon-Tyne, NE4 6AR; +44 191 272 1911; info@iskconnewcastle.org; iskconnewcastle.org

Rochester, England – Closet Krishna, 126 High Street, Rochester, ME1 1JT; +44 1634 81716; closetkrishna@aol.com; facebook.com/closetkrishna.charity

South Lanarkshire, Scotland – Krishna Eco Farm & Karuna Bhavan, Bankhouse Road, Lesmahagow, South Lanarkshire, ML11 0HQ; +44 7951 647438; info@iskconscotland.org; iskconscotland.org

Swansea, Wales ✦ The Hare Krishna Temple, 8 Cradock Street, Swansea, SA1 3EN; +44 1792 468469; info@iskconwales.org.uk; iskcon.swansea@pamho.net; iskconwales.org.uk

Upper Lough Erne, Northern Ireland – Krishna Island, Derrylin, Co. Fermanagh, BT92 9GN; +44 28677 23878; govindadvipa.info@gmail.com; krishnaisland.com

Watford, England – Bhaktivedanta Manor, Hilfield Lane, Herts, Watford, WD25 8EZ; +44 1923 851000; info@krishnatemple.com; krishnatemple.com

Watford, England ✧ GoKula Vegetarian Café, 65 Market Street, Watford, WD18 0PR; +44 1923 353289; facebook.com/GoKulaCafe

Other Countries

Auckland, New Zealand – 1229 Coatesville-Riverhead Highway, Kumeu 0892; +64 9 412 8075; facebook.com/nzharekrishna; harekrishna.org.nz

Barcelona, Spain – Plaza Real N 12, Entresuelo 2, 08002 Barcelona; +34 933 02 51 94; info@krishnabcn.com; krishnabcn.com

Budapest, Hungary – Lehel u. 15-17, 1039 Budapest; +36 1 391 04 35; info@krisna.hu; krisna.hu

Debrecen, Hungary ✦ Magyari u. 2, 4028 Debrecen; +36 30 372 99 59; info@harekrisna.hu; krisna.hu

Durban, South Africa ✦ 50 Bhaktivedanta Swami Circle, Westcliff, Chatsworth, Durban 4092; +27 31 403 3328; temple@iskcondurban.net; iskcondurban.net

Durbuy, Belgium ✦ Radhadesh, Château de Petite Somme, Durbuy, 6940 Septon; +32 86 32 29 26; info@radhadesh.com; radhadesh.com

Eger, Hungary ✦ Tűzoltó tér 5., 3300 Eger; +36 30 368 26 10; info@govindaeger.hu; krisna.hu

Jandelsbrunn, Germany – Simhachalam, Zielberg 20, 94118 Jandelsbrunn; +49 8583 316; info@simhachalam.de; simhachalam.de

Kathmandu, Nepal – Hare Krishna Dham, Budhanilkantha 5, Kathmandu, 44622; +977 1 4373790; info@iskconnepal.org; iskconnepal.org

Ljubljana, Slovenia – Žibertova 27, 1000 Ljubljana; +386 1 431 21 24; hkc.ljubljana@gmail.com; harekrisna.net

Los Angeles, USA ✦ 3764 Watseka Ave., Los Angeles, CA 90034; +1 310 836-2676; jagabeca@gmail.com; jagannivas.la@gmail.com; iskconla.com

Mayapur, India ✦ Shree Mayapur Chandrodaya Mandir, District Nadia, Shree Mayapur Dham, 741 313, West Bengal; +91 3472 245239, 245240, or 245233; mayapur.chandrodaya@pamho.net; mayapur.com

Melbourne, Australia – 197 Danks Street, Albert Park, Melbourne VIC 3206; +61 3 9699 5122; info@harekrishnamelbourne.com.au; harekrishnamelbourne.com.au

Moscow, Russia ✦ Kuusinena 19A, Moscow 125252; +7 925 772 62 95; info@krishna-temple.ru; krishna-temple.ru

Mumbai, India ✦ Hare Krishna Land, Juhu, Mumbai, 400 049, Maharashtra; +91 22 2620 6860; iskcon.juhu@pamho.net; guesthouse.mumbai@pamho.net; iskconmumbai.com

New Delhi, India ✦ Hare Krishna Hill, Sant Nagar Main Road, East of Kailash, New Delhi, 110 065, Uttar Pradesh; +91 11 2623 5133, 4, 5, 6, 7; delhi@pamho.net; guest.house.new.delhi@pamho.net; iskcondelhi.com

New York City, USA ✦ The Bhakti Center, 25 First Avenue, New York, NY 10003; +1 212 533-4842; info@bhakticenter.org; bhakticenter.org

Paris, France – 230 Avenue de la Division Leclerc, 95200 Sarcelles; +33 1 39 88 53 58; paris@pamho.net; www.iskcon.fr

Rio de Janeiro, Brazil – Estrada da Barra da Tijuca, 2010, Itanhangá, Rio de Janeiro, RJ 22641-004; +55 21 3563-1627; harekrishnarj.com.br

Rome, Italy – Via Sardegna 55, 00187 Roma; +39 06 6889 1540; info@harekrsna.it; harekrsna.it

Sarajevo, Bosnia-Herzegovina – Pofalicka Street no.11, 71000 Sarajevo; +387 33 973 088; iskcon.sarajevo@gmail.com

Somogyvámos, Hungary ✦ Krisna-völgy, Fő u. 38, 8699 Somogyvámos; +36 30 641 2309; +36 6 85 540 002; info@krisnavolgy.hu; krisnavolgy.hu

Stockholm, Sweden – New Radhakunda, Korsnäs Gård, 14792 Grödinge; +46 8 530 298 00; info@pamho.net; krishna.se

Sydney, Australia – 180 Falcon Street, North Sydney, Crows Nest NSW 2065; +61 2 9959 4558; info@iskcon.com.au; iskcon.com.au

Tenerife, Spain ✦ Vedic Cultural Centre, Rafael Puig Lluvina 32, C.C. Parque Santiago II, 330, 38660 Playa de las Américas; +34 635 172 411; info@iskcontenerife.es; iskcontenerife.es

Toronto, Canada – 243 Avenue Road, Toronto ON M5R 2J6; +1 416 922-5415; info@torontokrishna.com; torontokrishna.com

Vrindavan, India ✦ Krishna-Balaram Mandir, Bhaktivedanta Swami Marg, Raman Reti, Mathura, Vrindavan, 281121, Uttar Pradesh; +91 565 254 0021; info@iskconvrindavan.com; iskconvrindavan.com

Zagreb, Croatia – Ul. Bizek II 36, 10090 Zagreb; +385 99 806 40 29; zagreb@iskcon.hr; zagreb.iskcon.hr

Zurich, Switzerland – Krishna-Gemeinschaft Schweiz, Bergstrasse 54, 8032 Zürich; +41 44 262 33 88; kgs@krishna.ch; krishna.ch